"I was not prepared for how compelling this book is. It has all the ingredients of a spy thriller that will keep you turning the pages. Most of all, it is a testimony to the power, faithfulness and glory of the living God."

Dr. R. T. Kendall, senior minister (retired), Westminster Chapel, London

"This is an epic story. It spoke to me deeply. Hope for suffering servants flooded my soul as I received a fresh revelation of the heavenly Father's patient, long-suffering love. Everybody should read this and pass it on."

John Dawson, president emeritus, Youth With A Mission

"*Impossible Love* is faith building and motivating to an extreme, telling a story that will grip and strengthen every hungry heart that longs for God regardless of all opposition, pain and discouragement. This story gripped my heart as few books have and lifted me higher in Jesus than ever. Read it!"

Rolland and Heidi Baker, founding directors, Iris Global

"This book is powerful and unlike any other you have read. Craig's and Médine's stories couldn't be more different, yet God's impossible love weaves them together as they pursue Him. Reading this book kindled a flame in my heart to be a greater part of God's story, and I am sure you will also be changed by encountering the Author of Life in a fresh, new way."

Dr. Nabeel Qureshi, itinerant speaker, Ravi Zacharias International Ministries; *New York Times* bestselling author, *Seeking Allah, Finding Jesus*

"What happens when the world's greatest New Testament scholar pens his incredible story with his wife in riveting prose? You get *Impossible Love*. Captivating and candid, this is a sobering narrative on the merciful power of God to restore and bless in the face of insurmountable obstacles and suffering."

Frank Viola, author, *God's Favorite Place on Earth*, *The Day I Met Jesus* (with Mary DeMuth) and *Jesus: A Theography* (with Leonard Sweet); frankviola.org

"In my opinion, Craig Keener is one of the top five New Testament scholars in the world today. With *Impossible Love*, we get a glimpse of the man himself. But this book is no simple autobiography. It is a narrative filled with danger and tender love for God, seeking and standing courageously for Him in the midst of great sorrow, hardship and a sense of God's absence. If you want to see an example of two people who faced great hardships in life—while a supernatural God was always with them and delivered them to a life of fruitful love, joy and ministry—this is the book for you."

J. P. Moreland, distinguished professor of philosophy, Talbot School of Theology, Biola University; author, *The Soul: How We Know It's Real and Why It Matters*

"Dr. Craig Keener, brilliant biblical scholar, is known globally. *Impossible Love* introduces us to another Dr. Keener: Dr. Médine Moussounga Keener.

Impossible Love is not just the inspirational account of a love between a man and a woman. It is an open and welcoming window into God's grace that leaves the reader cheering while breathing a prayer of thanks for the goodness of God, who demonstrates His power most clearly in human weakness."

George O. Wood, general superintendent, General Council of the Assemblies of God

"*Impossible Love* is the kind of book we all need to read—to remind ourselves of the reality of God, His power and the way He supernaturally intersects our lives. This book changed my perspective on the power of God in the lives of His people."

Mary DeMuth, author, *Worth Living: How God's Wild Love for You Makes You Worthy*

"What an incredible story! This amazing book is a real page-turner, full of hope and the character of Jesus in the midst of incredible challenges—and with a happy ending at that."

Dr. Michael L. Brown, host, nationally syndicated daily radio show *The Line of Fire*

"A genuinely epic encounter of two people coming together from two different parts of the world experiencing God's grace in overcoming unspeakable obstacles. This is biographical testimony at its best because it is not merely a story of two people, but the story of God's prevailing work in our lives."

Timothy C. Tennent, Ph.D., president, Asbury Theological Seminary

"An epic love story that takes place in a time of war—a love story not just between Craig and Médine Keener but between God and His people. If you have ever wondered where God is in the midst of suffering and loss, you must read *Impossible Love*! This is one of those rarest of books that inspires me to pray to want to know and love God better."

Rich Nathan, author; senior pastor, Vineyard Columbus

"Packed with drama, adventure, danger, faith and hope. Be ready to experience a real-life story more incredible than any work of fiction. You'll be inspired and encouraged by Craig and Médine's story of impossible love."

J. Warner Wallace, cold-case detective; author, *Cold-Case Christianity* and *God's Crime Scene*

"*Impossible Love* has it all: conflict of civil war, danger, love, friendship, faith, miracles, deliverance supernaturally and the presentation of the faithfulness of God. I highly recommend it to all."

Randy Clark, overseer, Apostolic Network of Global Awakening; author, *There Is More!*, *The Essential Guide to Healing* (with Bill Johnson), *The Healing Breakthrough*

IMPOSSIBLE LOVE

IMPOSSIBLE LOVE

The TRUE STORY *of an* AFRICAN CIVIL WAR,
MIRACLES *and* HOPE AGAINST ALL ODDS

CRAIG S. KEENER *and*
MÉDINE MOUSSOUNGA KEENER

Chosen
a division of Baker Publishing Group
Minneapolis, Minnesota

Published by Chosen Books
11400 Hampshire Avenue South
Bloomington, Minnesota 55438
www.chosenbooks.com

Chosen Books is a division of
Baker Publishing Group, Grand Rapids, Michigan

Printed in the United States of America

Library of Congress Cataloging-in-Publication Data

Names: Keener, Craig S., author.
Title: Impossible love : the true story of an African civil war, miracles, and hope against all hope / Craig Keener and Médine Moussounga Keener.
Description: Minneapolis, Minnesota : Chosen, 2016.
Identifiers: LCCN 2015038583 | ISBN 9780800797775 (pbk. : alk. paper)
Subjects: LCSH: Keener, Craig S., 1960- | Keener, Médine Moussounga. | Christian biography--Africa. | Christian biography--United States.
Classification: LCC BR1700.3 .K44 2016 | DDC 270.8/30922--dc23 LC record available at http://lccn.loc.gov/2015038583

Scripture translations are provided by the author.

Some names have been changed in this story to protect individual privacy or safety. The following are pseudonyms: Maitre Bouka; Cass; Estelle; Manassé; Massala; Matai; Samuel Malonga; Oswardo; Raphael; and Zonzon.

Cover design by Dual Identity

16 17 18 19 20 21 22   7 6 5 4 3 2 1

In keeping with biblical principles of creation stewardship, Baker Publishing Group advocates the responsible use of our natural resources. As a member of the Green Press Initiative, our company uses recycled paper when possible. The text paper of this book is composed in part of post-consumer waste.

Lovingly dedicated
to the memory of Mama Jacques
(Antoinette Malombé)
and Papa Jacques Moussounga

Republic of the Congo
(Congo-Brazzaville)

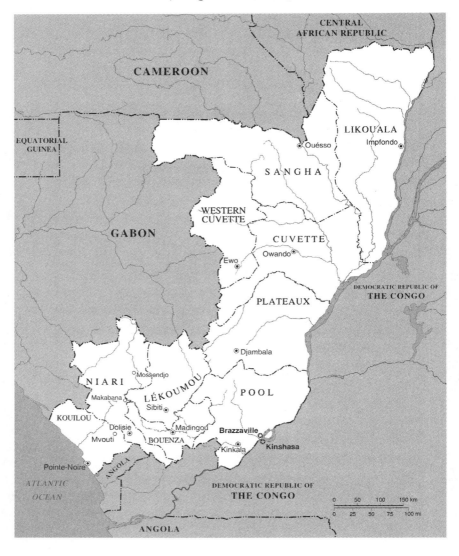

Contents

Contents

Preface

Sixteen-month-old David, strapped to my back, sang exuberantly, as if celebrating the angry barrage of nearby gunfire and explosions. Whether he was enjoying the noise or acting oblivious to it, he was the only person in our small party of fugitives who could do either.

We were the last stragglers to abandon our neighborhood. A relative was pushing my disabled father, known to everyone as Papa Jacques, in a frail old green wheelbarrow. Although some fugitives had felt forced to leave aged or sick relatives behind, we would never have left without my father. That was why we had remained so long, even after members of the southern militia, the soldiers from our region, had warned all civilians to leave. Now our city, Dolisie, in western Congo, Central Africa, was burning behind us.

As my family and I trekked the dirt road up the hill, struggling with baggage on our heads, my mind wandered to a very different time, when I was finishing my Ph.D. in the West. That was where I had met my closest Western friend, Craig. Our affection

11

for each other had not translated into successful romance, but we had remained intimate friends. We often confided our hearts to each other, as a close brother and sister would. That was why, despite the danger of discussing the political situation of a civil war, I had found someone leaving the country and sent Craig a letter a month before the city fell. I knew that if my letter reached him, he would never stop praying until he learned of my fate.

My mother's shriek cut into my thoughts.

Thérèse, my big sister, spoke, her words little more than a gasp. "What is it, Mama Jacques?"

My mother raised her hands to her face. "In our hurry to escape, I forgot Papa Jacques's medicines—I left them on the table."

I felt sick as she spoke. Papa Jacques could not survive long without his medicines.

"I've got to go back," Mama Jacques said.

Thérèse shook her head. "No, no! It's safer for me to go back."

My heart jumped. "No—let me go. Because I have my baby on my back, I'm the least likely to be raped or killed if found alone."

We stood as though frozen. What should we do? We knew that other fugitives who had returned to their towns for forgotten items had been killed. And yet every moment that we delayed in this open place put us in greater danger from marksmen.

I could not imagine how we could all survive our situation. Nor could I imagine what the days that followed this one would bring. But before I tell you all that occurred in my life as a fugitive, Craig and I want to recount the events that led up to it. Craig will tell more of his story before I tell most of mine. Nevertheless, this is the story of two people struggling to hold on to the belief that God's heart was bigger than our pain.

Two people longing for closeness, but separated by continents, cultures, government regulations and war. But two people who believed that faith, hope and love can surmount even the most overwhelming obstacles.

Come with us back to the beginning and let us tell you about this impossible love.

1

Keep Walking

Craig

"Keep on walkin'," the middle-aged man barked in my direction. He was slouched on a downtown park bench some thirty feet away from me. The night was dark and quiet apart from the streetlights and our two voices.

"Sure, sir, I will," I promised, "but I just want to tell you first that Jesus loves you."

While attending a Bible college in Missouri, I was volunteering at Victory Mission, a Christian ministry that served food to homeless people. Everett and Esther Cook, retired church planters and directors of the mission, were funding the ministry through their retirement income. In my work there during the previous two weeks, I had led someone to faith in Christ each week. In fact, in various settings through the previous four years since my conversion, forty or fifty people had prayed with me to commit their lives to Christ.

I was hoping that I would be able to share my faith with someone in the same way this night, even though Brother Cook had warned me not to go. "It's going to be dangerous out there tonight," he told me.

Brother Cook and Sister Cook were rarely misguided in hearing God's leading, but I figured that danger on the street was nothing new. Sometimes the homeless people we worked with were beaten or killed; in two cases, the bodies were not found until the next morning. In my youth and inexperience, I could not imagine why one night would be any more dangerous than any other.

"I'll be fine," I insisted, and brushed past Brother Cook on my way out. I should have known better.

"I told you to keep on walkin'!" the man shouted, springing from his bench with clenched fists. He lunged at me so quickly that I barely had time to realize what was happening.

He began pummeling my face as I protested, bewildered. "Sir, why are you doing this? I haven't done anything to you." Ultimately his motives mattered less to me than his rage. I kept backing up, unable to evade his kicks and violent blows.

I felt my marked-up Bible, my constant companion, starting to slip from my hand. It was well worn, with many loose pages. I realized that if it fell and I stooped to pick it up, this man had the strength to knock me to the ground and kick me to death. I clutched my Bible as hard as I could while trying to protect my face.

I had been beaten for my witnessing twice before in another part of the country and ended up on the ground, with my aggressor ripping out my hair and repeatedly slamming my head down. In those instances, bystanders had pulled my attackers off me. But this time the street, though well lit, looked abandoned.

Survival instincts drowned out the rising pain in my body, especially my face. I kept backing my way toward a side street.

Once I reached it, I turned and walked away as quickly as my aching legs allowed. I felt ashamed, as if I were a coward; although I was not literally running away, I was valuing my survival more than sharing my faith. The angry man did not pursue me.

"If I ever see you again," he shouted, "I'll kill you!"

Before returning to the mission, I stopped in front of a store window near a streetlight. I wiped blood from my face and hoped that I could look inconspicuous as I entered the mission. Brother Cook, however, was leaning against the doorway.

"Dangerous out there tonight, isn't it?" he said.

"Everything's fine," I retorted, slipping past him quickly. The next day I had two black eyes, but I never did tell him what happened that night.

An Atheist Meets God

I had not always been zealous for my faith. I did not grow up in church in my small Ohio town; I was, in fact, a convinced atheist by age nine. My family was intellectual; my father a hardworking man of integrity, my mother creative and affirming of all my childhood intellectual pursuits. But we did not discuss religion much. When Christians started sharing their faith with me, even though I was young, I would ridicule them or use what I knew of science and philosophy to try to expose flaws in their arguments.

Ironically, what began to call my atheist certainties into question was reading Plato when I was thirteen. His arguments did not particularly appeal to me, but his questions got me thinking: *What happens after we die? If there is nothing higher than ourselves, then is life just a fleeting, meaningless accident?* The stakes were high, and as years passed I began secretly to question my atheism. "God, if You're out there," I began to plead, "please show me."

One day two fundamentalist Baptists wearing suits and ties stopped me on my way home from school. "Do you know where you'll go when you die?" one demanded. That question grabbed my attention, though at first I thought he was taking a survey.

"Probably either heaven or hell," I joked, assuming that he was a Christian. I thought that almost everyone was a Christian, which was one reason that I was not. It looked to me as though most people did not take their faith seriously; surely those who genuinely believed that God had created them would devote their entire lives to pleasing Him.

Unamused, my questioners launched into a series of Bible verses designed to show me how I could go to heaven. Jesus died so I could be forgiven, they explained. He rose again so that if I trusted in Him, I could have eternal life. I tried to listen patiently this time, but finally I cut off the more vocal of the two.

"Sir, I'm sorry, but quoting the Bible can't persuade me. I'm an atheist. I don't believe in the Bible. Do you have any other arguments?"

They exchanged uncomfortable glances, as if caught off guard.

Seeing that they had nothing else to offer, I pressed my ultimate objection against their faith. "If there's a God," I protested, "then where did the dinosaur bones come from?"

If you ask a stupid question, you get a stupid answer. At the time I did not know that Christians hold a range of views about such subjects; nor did these evangelists inform me.

After a moment of silence, the more vocal speaker said, "The devil put them there to confuse us." His partner hesitated briefly at this pronouncement, then nodded vigorously.

I should not have expected street preachers to be experts on paleontology, but his answer appeared so ridiculous that I shrugged them off, exasperated. "I'm leaving," I said and turned to go.

"Your heart will grow harder every time you reject Christ," he called solemnly after me. "And you'll end up burning in hell forever."

The Presence

Normally this is not the way that Christians recommend expressing Christ's love. Yet as I walked home, I trembled. I began to feel an unexplainable presence, something I had never felt during my studies of various philosophies or religions. I had been asking God to reveal Himself to me, but I had expected scientific evidence. Instead He gave me evidence more personally compelling: He gave me evidence of His own presence.

My home offered no defense against this demanding Presence. I went into my bedroom and shut the door. If God was real, then my supposed intellectual superiority over Christians was wrong. In fact, I was utterly at God's mercy. If I rejected the Presence now, I did not know that He would give me another chance. My heart raced between my two options as I paced in my room for perhaps as much as half an hour. Finally I could not hold out any longer.

"God, I don't understand how Jesus' death and resurrection can restore me to You," I gasped desperately. "But if that's what You're saying, I'll believe it."

The presence was so strong now that my knees buckled under me. "But God, I don't know how to be restored to You," I whispered. "So if You really want me to belong to You, You're going to have to restore me Yourself."

I felt something rushing through my body, a feeling like nothing I had ever experienced before. I jumped up, astonished. I did not know much about Christianity, and some of what I thought I knew was wrong. But I now knew one thing: God was real, and He was found in Christ. And I knew that from that moment on I wanted to devote everything to Him.

That experience proved only the beginning of many surprises for me. In the days and early years that followed, I found in God a love and intimacy deeper than any I had ever expected, a love that seemed impossible to humanly imagine.

2

Sharing the Faith

Craig

I had never experienced the Good News of God's saving love until the day of my conversion, and I wanted to make sure that no one else suffered the same misfortune. Sometimes, because I spent so much time talking with people about Christ, the half-hour walk home from school took me four hours.

Not everyone was eager to talk. Once I approached some men who were smoking pot. When I started telling them about Christ, one of them rebuffed me by saying, "Go away, man, we're sinning." Another time I was working at a car wash and started sharing my faith with a carload of men. One of them blurted, "Oh, man, I remember you." It was the same guys. Sometimes I shared Christ with people as they were getting drunk or smoking pot. I did learn, however, that it is usually easier to reason with people about Christ when they are not stoned.

While the pastor of the church I joined mentored me the most, ministers from various churches in town gave me advice and mentored me, while friends from different churches sometimes teamed up with me in sharing our faith. One was an African American friend named Kyrk Freeman. When we started witnessing to each other one day, we discovered that both of us had recently been converted. His family always welcomed me as if I were a member of their own family, and we often visited each other's churches. Years later I learned that some of the young people I had led to Christ or discipled in his neighborhood still remembered me.

Not everybody liked us sharing our faith. People often ridiculed me, one guy pulled a knife on me, and another guy beat me while I kept preaching. But so convinced was I that Jesus is the source of life, I was prepared to die for His honor.

Falling in Love

It was disconcerting to realize that the little children in Sunday school knew the Bible better than I did. Desperate for more knowledge, I began reading forty chapters of the Bible a day for weeks at a time.

As I read about God speaking to people, I wondered why He no longer spoke today. I experienced feelings and impressions, some of which seemed to be God's leading, but others reflected indigestion. Yet I longed to hear from God. As I was out walking on a mostly deserted road one day, I sensed that God was giving me faith to believe that He would grant me what I so deeply yearned for, so I asked: "God, please open my ears to hear Your voice."

In that moment, I heard such deep love that it astonished me. I had assumed that God would be angry with me, but instead He spoke tenderly: *My child, for so long I've desired to show you how much I love you. But you're wrapped up in all the things you're trying to do for Me, while you're afraid of My presence.*

I had never experienced such deep love before. I longed for God's voice so much that each day I would go out again along that deserted road to walk and listen to what He would say, and sometimes to write the songs He gave me. I realized that no one could come to know what God was truly like without falling madly in love with Him.

It was my first time being in love. One day, like a dreamy adolescent, I asked God, "How much do You love me?"

Look at the cross, My child, He answered. *Look at the nails in Jesus' hands, the thorns in His brow, the spear in His side, and see the blood. My child,* that's *how much I love you.*

The Bible was clear that our relationship with God starts with His love in the cross, not our works. For a time I had grown so preoccupied with trying to be properly religious that I had become afraid of intimacy with Him. Gradually, though, as I kept hearing about the depth of God's love for His people, I began to understand a little better how much He longs for us to love Him and one another.

Sometimes I also heard His sorrow. One night, after I had experienced a broken relationship that wounded my heart, I felt Jesus' presence particularly deeply. *I know how it feels to experience sorrow,* I felt Him say. *All My disciples left Me and fled. Even now, when My heart breaks for the world's need, My people are more concerned with their own business than they are with what matters to Me—other people.*

I discovered that a broken heart can help us to feel what matters to God, whose heart breaks for the world. The Bible says that He is near the broken and the lowly. His presence was so near that I told Him I was willing to experience far more brokenness, so long as I could always experience His presence to go with it.

Bible College

Because I felt that my intellect had led me astray before my conversion, I questioned initially whether or not I should go to college. Finally I sensed that God was leading me to go to Bible college; when I turned down a potential National Merit Scholarship because it would not cover Bible colleges, almost everyone thought I was crazy. After a summer of work, I set out for Missouri without even sufficient funds to pay for my full first semester.

When Bible college started, I was fasting two days a week, praying for God's work on the campus. Although I had grown more cautious about listening to God's voice, sometimes I heard things that made no sense to me. One evening early in my freshman year, for example, I was trying to study but kept getting distracted, as if God was telling me something for another freshman named Leslie. Specifically I felt as though He wanted me to tell her that she was allowed to date, which in our circles meant a friendly relationship exploring the possibility of marriage. Personally I did not believe in dating; I thought people should just wait to hear from God about whom to marry.

Finally the impression felt so overwhelming that I asked to meet with her briefly. "I feel as though God is telling me something for you," I prefaced, "but I don't personally agree with it." Naturally she looked skeptical, but she waited, so I proceeded. "I feel He's saying that you're allowed to date."

She seemed stunned and at a loss for words for a few moments. "I haven't told anyone on campus this," she said finally, "but before my conversion I was divorced. I've been secretly asking God if I could date and someday marry."

Ah, I thought, *that explains what this was about.* Relieved, I went back to my homework. I did not know her circumstances, but surely God would not hold anyone's preconversion divorce against him or her any more than any other preconversion sin—my atheism, for example. When I discovered how some divorced Christians were treated, even when they had been abandoned against their will, I resolved to speak in their defense someday. Still, I was not in a position to understand their pain myself.

Real Life Begins

It was during my time at Bible college that I helped at the local street mission run by the Cooks. I also eventually fell in love with a fellow student whom I will call Cass. We prayed together, studied together and witnessed together. Each of us had a difficult background, but I was certain that God could restore anyone. Cass was the one person I would trust unreservedly. By then Brother Cook had died, so Cass and I met with Sister Cook, who was also known for listening to God. When she prayed with us, she warned us that something difficult lay ahead. It sounded scary, but eventually we forgot her warning.

After I graduated, Cass returned home to work, and I began master's work in history and religion at what is today Missouri State University. The only job I could find was in a fast-food restaurant, so I often walked the five miles to and from the university, even at night, to avoid the fifty-cent bus fare. I also ate simply; though I am nearly six feet tall, sometimes I weighed just 132 pounds.

I began pastoring a multiethnic congregation that was too small to offer a salary. I fasted a day each week to pray for God's transforming power in the message I would give that week. Idealistic, I imagined that after my first ten sermons the handful of people in the congregation would be so zealous for God that a nationwide revival would break out. I was the one who had the most to learn.

25

I heard God's brokenhearted love deeply in prophetic parts of the Bible, especially Jeremiah and Hosea. I felt His lament that much of the Church in America was unfaithful; also that we were arrogant, feeling that we were somehow immune to what Christians were suffering elsewhere in the world. *I will strip them of the things they value,* I felt Him warn, *so they may learn to value what really matters.*

The one time Cass was able to visit me in Missouri was the week that I gave a play—a monologue—from the book of Hosea. That book communicated deeply God's heart of love and faithfulness without compromising His holiness. As Hosea's wife betrayed him, so God's people betrayed Him; yet God still loved them and wanted them back. As I delivered that play to my little congregation, I could almost feel God's brokenhearted pain for the world.

Ministry on the Street

Ministry on the street continued. One week I was sharing my faith with a man on Flatbush Avenue in Brooklyn when he grew angry and tapped something inside his coat.

"You talk about heaven," he said. "I'll see how ready you are to go to heaven. I've got a gun here. I'm gonna blow your brains out. Then we'll see how ready you are for heaven."

My heart was racing; guns were typically more lethal than beatings. I did not doubt that I would go to heaven, but what about my calling that I kept feeling to bring the Church back to the Scriptures? Obviously I was not fulfilling it yet, since I did not even understand what it meant.

"If you shoot me, I'll go to heaven," I answered much more calmly than I felt. "But I'd prefer to stay here longer so I can keep sharing Christ with people like yourself, people whom God loves."

He backed up. "Yeah, you're just scared," he said, turning away.

Though a wiser person might have been satisfied with his departure, I did not want him to get the wrong idea. "I *am* ready to go to heaven," I countered as he strode off.

The next night on the same street, that man found me and apologized. "Hey, man, sorry about last night. I was a little drunk. But I talked it over with my wife, and we want to come visit your church."

I was too elated to ask him if he had really had a gun.

3

From Africa
to the United States

Médine

When I was growing up, my country felt secure. Although I was sorry for the Ethiopian refugees I saw, their plight was not something that could happen in our country.

I grew up in a home that was devoted to God. My father had read that Medina was considered a holy city, so he named me after that city. He did not know that it was not a Christian city. Both my parents had converted to Christianity from traditional African religions, and both loved Jesus. My father was my hero—always generous, always joyfully helping others.

Although my father wanted to be a pastor, he worked for the railroad company. There he worked to eliminate corruption and made the railroad safer. His job also provided opportunities to serve God by starting and reviving churches in different villages and towns. He could do the Lord's work without having to charge anyone for it.

My closest brother, Emmanuel, was like my father. Emmanuel earned his Ph.D. in chemistry. He was brilliant and made some new pharmaceutical discoveries, though his mentor got the public credit. We were very close as children—Emmanuel, my younger brothers, Aimé and Eliser, my sisters, Thérèse and Gracia, and I. Because I grew up in a family-oriented culture, my story is as much about them as about myself.

Answered Prayers

Much of Africa lacks adequate medical resources, causing untold suffering. At the same time, God sometimes hears desperate prayers. One day when my big sister, Thérèse, was about two years old, my mother heard her scream a dreaded word: "Snake!" She raced to Thérèse's side only to find her not breathing.

Weeping, my mother strapped the lifeless body of her child to her back and ran up and down hills for perhaps three hours until she reached the village where my father's friend Coco Moïse was doing ministry. Moïse examined the still form.

"We'll pray," he announced solemnly. As soon as he finished praying, Thérèse began breathing again.

People were also often healed when my father would pray. My younger sister, Gracia, was dying of meningitis. The French doctor at the clinic warned sadly that she would not survive the night. Desperate, Papa Jacques prayed beside his comatose daughter all night long. In the morning light, the physician was surprised to discover Gracia not only alive but conscious. The nurse, a nun, declared it a miracle.

Likewise one time I was very sick with a fever that would not go away. After this continued for many days, my father returned from work to find me very weak.

He prayed, "Dear God, heal Médine, in Jesus' name, Amen."

Then he looked straight into my eyes and asked, "Do you trust me?"

"Of course," I responded.

"Do you trust God?"

"Certainly."

"Then go and pour water on yourself," he said.

I hesitated; I already had chills, and by this time of day the water was cold. But I trusted my father. As soon as my hand touched the water, I was instantly healed.

When I was about five years old, Coco Moïse saw me in a vision.

"Médine is like a star," he said. "She'll go to a far country, study for a long time and then come back here. But there will be war here when she's coming back. I see her arriving at the airport . . . but now I can't see her because of bombing."

My parents were alarmed and for several weeks continued praying for my safety.

Struggles

Despite periodic miracles, life was hard. One night during a power outage, for example, as we children were playing in our bedroom, a long snake slithered unseen toward us. Papa Jacques happened to return home just in time. Holding the flashlight that had guided his walk home, he spotted the snake and beat it to death before it could strike.

We had to walk long distances to school. Children disappeared in those days. Boys' bodies were sometimes recovered with their hearts missing, used for occult sacrifices; one of my cousins was nearly abducted this way. Far more often, girls were raped by teachers or by relatives. My sisters and I evaded several rape attempts over the years, grateful for our parents' prayers.

Even more disconcerting, Papa Jacques was sometimes targeted for assassination. Because he was one of the leaders in the rail workers' labor union, some assumed that he was involved in politics, even though he was not. During one period, we were not supposed to answer the phone. One time I forgot about the danger and answered our phone. "Yes, he's here," I said. My father quickly put the phone down; he could have been killed, and I was terrified.

On another occasion, a military man kept coming by our house and finding my father away, or going to my father's workplace and hearing that he had left for home. Three years later the man arrived in Dolisie and noticed the train station nicely repaired.

"What happened here?" the man inquired.

"Moussounga Jacques improved our station," the worker responded proudly.

"Oh! I didn't know he had moved here. May I see his office?"

Now, for the first time, the military man came face to face with Papa Jacques. "Please, sit down, sir," my father invited him politely.

The man cut straight to the point. "Who's your witchdoctor?" he demanded. "Who's protecting you?"

"What are you talking about?" Papa Jacques asked, confused.

The man laughed. "Three years ago your neighbor hired me to kill you," he said. Papa Jacques's blood ran cold as the assassin continued. "I never found you, and when I retired last year I gave up. In my experience people don't just elude me like that. So tell me, who gave you this kind of protection?"

Papa Jacques paused and then leaned back in his seat, a smile spreading over his face. "Let me tell you about Him," he began.

University in Congo

Attending our country's university brought another challenge. Everyone there knew that my brother Emmanuel and I were Christians; we took in students who were hungry and did not have safe places to stay. Some people made fun of me, but I shared my faith freely.

Corruption was widespread. Teachers often demanded sex from students as a precondition for passing classes. Written exams were graded blind, but one teacher threatened to fail me on my oral exam if I did not sleep with him. Although I was afraid I would fail, I would not compromise. By God's grace, each time oral exams were given I was assigned to a different professor.

I wanted to study for a master's degree in English in the United States. Because I ranked third in the university in English study, I was awarded the required scholarship. Some professors, however, misappropriated the scholarship money. I then applied for a government scholarship to attend the University of Lille in France; I did not know that officials often required bribes, but I would not have paid one anyway. I kept going to ask about the scholarship, day after day, until finally the officer, wearied, ordered, "Put her name on the list."

Finally the departure date came. Some students who had scholarships discovered that government ministers had replaced their names with those of people they preferred. As names were called, some hardworking students whose names had been crossed off began crying. My name, however, remained. A government worker who recognized me was shocked.

"Which official helped you?" he asked.

"The big one," I answered happily. "Jesus."

That evening Papa Jacques wanted to see me off at the airport. He was not an official, but he entered the airport with such dignity that the workers assumed he was and let him stay.

Prejudice in France

My scholarship covered the cost of my classes, but I arrived in France without food or money. It was winter and I was shivering; I had no warm clothes. Only my new church family made me feel at home.

Classes had started October 15. Because our country had delayed sending us, it was now December 1. "Another African," the director of the business English section complained upon my arrival. In class he would declare that whites are more intelligent than blacks.

When the time came to defend my master's thesis a year later, he kept delaying the date. Finally I was able to complete all of my requirements for my degree and applied for doctoral study at University of Paris 7. On a cold February day I made my way to the registrar's office and submitted my request to register. But the registrar shook her head. "Your visa can't be renewed," she said in a curt voice. "You waited too long to apply after finishing your master's thesis."

I did not know what she was talking about. "I just defended my thesis in January," I protested.

"I'm sorry," the registrar responded, "but your document shows that you defended in October, not January. For an October defense, you should have renewed your identification in November."

Her charge caught me totally off guard. "But—it *was* January."

"Young lady, you're lying. Don't expect me to take your word against that of your professor."

I stumbled out of the office. To ensure the end of my academic career, my professor had falsified the date. Now it was my word against that of a white professor. I was going to have to return to Congo with no further chance to study abroad. Ashamed and frustrated, I found my way to the Seine River, sat down and sobbed for half an hour.

As I was praying there, however, I suddenly remembered that I had with me my professor's letter inviting me to defend my thesis—and it had the January date. I rushed back to the registrar's office, arriving ten minutes before it closed. As the registrar examined the letter, she turned red. The professor had been the one lying!

"I'm going to help you," the registrar promised.

Because I excelled in my work, I was soon given entry into the Ph.D. program.

Still, life as an international student was challenging. Sometimes finances were so tight that I lived on bread and water. I also had to commute three days every week for classes, with my train returning around 10:30 at night. Walking through drug-infested neighborhoods to reach home by midnight, I prayed hard. One night someone pulled down his trousers and I ran to escape him, but most nights passed uneventfully.

Approved for another scholarship, I was given the opportunity to fulfill my dream to study in the United States. I would do the research there for my doctoral dissertation. There I would also meet a young man whose Christian joy was strangely laced with sorrow. From the day we met I mused that I had never met someone so devoted to Christ who was also so sad. He carried the wounds of a tragedy that I could not yet understand.

4

Rejection

Craig

Cass and I were married in a big wedding full of promise. Each of us worked when work was available, but for our first three years of marriage and school, we lived in the only place we could afford: a cockroach-infested basement apartment. The carpet would stink for a week whenever heavy rains flooded our apartment.

Ministry was hard, work was demanding, and we lacked money for adequate medical care and sometimes ample food. The one thing we counted on was each other's love and our plans together for future ministry.

Changing Values

I had always associated the term *holiness* with legalism—in dress codes and intellectual freedom. But one day in prayer I sensed God saying this: *Holiness is like a consuming fire.*

Holiness is loving Me so much that nothing else matters compared to Me.

"I love You more than anything," I affirmed happily, and began pursuing God more deeply, continuously overcoming heart temptations rather than excusing them.

I often preached to my little congregation that real followers of Christ owe God not just Sunday mornings or a tithe, but everything we are and everything we have. Some of those I pastored complained that my own view of holiness was legalistic.

"God doesn't expect you to serve Him in *everything* you do," they argued.

Unable to dissuade me, they began placing pressure on Cass. In time Cass began to express her agreement with those individuals who wanted to keep certain interests or desires separate from their faith. I gave up trying to convince her of my values, but I could not change what I believed. One day she revealed how wide the gap between us had become.

"I'm thinking of turning away from God," she announced.

I was horrified. I watched desperately as her behavior began to change. She grew distant and stayed away from home more and more. In prayer I heard God telling me that she was being unfaithful. I presumed that He meant this figuratively.

Soon, however, it became clear that God meant it literally. Cass announced one day that she was going away for the weekend. When she returned home early Monday morning I knew somehow what had happened, and with whom.

Although she looked as though she had not had much sleep, Cass entered the apartment in a hurry to get ready for work.

"Cass," I began, "did you spend the weekend with Oswardo?"

Oswardo was a close friend, and his wife, Estelle, was Cass's closest friend in our city. I knew that Oswardo had been away that weekend. I also knew that he was rumored to have had affairs.

"No," she said, her voice cold.

"Cass, I want to let you know that even if you did, I love you and forgive you. I just want you back."

"That's nice," she growled. "Now if you'll excuse me, I don't want to see you right now."

I was devastated. I could barely move through the day. Later in the afternoon she asked me to sit down and listen to what she had to say.

"I know you love me," she began, "and I'm sorry this hurts you, but I'm not sorry for what I'm doing. I didn't want to get Oswardo in trouble with Estelle, but now that he's told her, I can tell you. I'm *going* to leave you, Craig, as soon as I have the money to get my own apartment. And after that, I'll file for divorce."

I wept and pleaded with her, but for perhaps the first time in our marriage, she was too cold to bend at all.

"I never knew what love was until I met Oswardo," she gushed.

Those words stung deeply. I could not believe them. I loved her with all my heart and could not believe that our marriage was dead or that she had gone this far. And while I had always had compassion for those who face divorce, I had never even slightly imagined that divorce could happen to *me*.

God's Spirit often assured me that I was His child, just as Paul says: "The Spirit himself testifies with our spirit that we are God's children" (Romans 8:16). But if I was following God's daily leading as His child, how could I have missed Him about whom to marry? Granted that Cass had free will, and Christians do suffer; surely God had known the future. Would He have led me into such a situation? Yet even if I could not hear Him accurately, surely He could hear me. I had prayed and believed sincerely that He would lead me to the right marriage partner.

Where was God in all this? Had He not called me? Had I sinned against Him so gravely that He had abandoned me? My faith was shattered. My life now felt horribly surreal, beyond my worst nightmare. I felt like a twig being bent in God's hand, ready to snap. I knew that God promises to work all things for good to those who love Him, but what if my love for Him could not hold out that long?

Sleepless Nights

Cass refused to sleep in bed with me, so I threw a blanket onto the couch and tried to rest. It was no use; I was too anguished to sleep. I got dressed and went outside to pray, wandering through one neighborhood after the other. At about two in the morning, a police officer pulled his car over beside where I was on the sidewalk.

"Someone reported a stranger in the neighborhood," he said, "so I just need to check what you're doing."

My heart sank further. "My wife is leaving me," I said, my head hung low. "I can't sleep. I had to get out and pray."

The officer's face softened. "Man, I'm sorry. I went through that a year ago. You keep walking."

God was silent. But as I kept taking one step after another, His voice finally broke through, taking me to the heart of what my experience was really about. I am not always sure of everything that I hear in prayer, but I am sure I heard God that night.

Cass didn't do anything to you and Hosea's wife didn't do anything to him that My people haven't done to Me again and again, He said, His voice heavy with sorrow. *Day and night I call to them from the deepest love, but day and night they are too consumed with all the other things they love more than they love Me.*

As He spoke, I felt more than ever Hosea's broken heart—the broken heart of God. I saw how so much of what we pour our time into—our entertainment and friends and fun and even our religious activities—often obscures what matters most: His love.

A few days later I was able to talk with Oswardo. He said that he felt ashamed. I was able to speak what was in my heart gently and without anger, yet firmly. "My friend," I said, "I love you and I forgive you. But you must stay away from my wife."

Estelle was devastated as well. She seemed desperate to preserve her own marriage, though she had little love now for Cass.

Breaking Up?

A good friend, Henry Morse, my successor for the little congregation I had pastored until a year before, began working with Oswardo. At one point Henry felt a divine urgency such as he had never felt before.

"Oswardo," Henry said, "you need to break off the relationship by phone."

"I need to break it off in person," Oswardo said. "I owe her that, bro."

"This isn't some godly relationship that deserves a gentle funeral," Henry warned. "I feel God saying that if you meet with her in person, you'll never be free from this."

A few days later, however, Oswardo and Cass were both "missing." Estelle called me, panicked; Henry was out looking for them.

I was too broken to put up a fight. "Just pray, Estelle," I told her. "God is the only one who can help us now."

I went to walk through the woods to pray—and when I emerged I walked right into Cass and Oswardo! I could not believe it. I was certain that God must have led me to them.

"Come on, Cass, let's go," I said, grabbing her hand.

Cass shook me off. "You were spying on us!" she seethed.

Oswardo, by contrast, sounded contrite. "It's all right, bro," he explained. "We're just breaking up." He handed me a note of apology. I stared at the words on the paper.

"You were warned through prophecy not to do it this way," I said, looking up at him.

"Henry told me that, bro," Oswardo explained, "but it wasn't a prophecy. That was just his opinion."

Cass would not come with me, so I went home. Oswardo was not doing it the right way, but at least they were breaking up. That meant there was hope for our marriages.

Once I reached the apartment I called Estelle. "I, uh, found them," I said.

"Where? Where?" she demanded desperately, choking with tears.

"It's all right," I offered prematurely. "They're breaking up."

When Cass returned home, the only thing I knew to do was try to acknowledge the hurt I supposed she felt over the breakup of her relationship with Oswardo. Even with all the pain I was feeling, I loved her and did not want to see her suffer.

She responded to my effort at kindness with curses. "If you and Estelle were just dead," she shouted, "my relationship with Oswardo would be all right."

Foolishly, I tried to touch her arm. She began flailing at me and screaming at me to get out. I blocked the physical blows with my arms; my heart, however, bore their full force. I left the apartment.

The next day I was finally able to get her to talk with me. I knew she was in pain and offered to listen.

"Share your hurt with me," I said. This time my words must have touched her. She spoke slowly, as if she was unsure of how to explain things to me.

"I can't tell you how I feel about this," she said. "You're my husband."

"But I was your friend before I was your husband," I said. "And you really need a friend right now."

My few counseling classes had taught me to reflect feelings. I thus tried to listen as sensitively as possible as, for two hours, she poured out her hurt about Oswardo. He was handsome and muscular, unlike me. He did not have acne on his back, like me. As for me, I was gentle and loving, but awkward and introverted.

"Even though I want Oswardo," she concluded, "I never really wanted to hurt you."

"I'm not the handsomest or richest man in the world," I promised her, "but you'll never find someone more faithful than I."

She finally softened. "I know you love me," she said, her voice now gentle. "Even though I love Oswardo, you would've always been my second choice. If Oswardo doesn't come back to me, I'll probably come back to you."

I was actually overjoyed at this unflattering declaration. Maybe God could give us a second chance.

Last Chances

The reprieve proved mercilessly temporary. The next day I left a rose on the table; I found it in the trash. A couple of mornings later I felt an unusual urge to go by the YMCA where Cass was working out. I arrived to find Oswardo waiting outside in his car.

"I promised Estelle not to go inside if I saw Cass's car here," he explained hastily.

"Oswardo—let's go somewhere to talk," I urged. He drove us to the university, and I kept him busy talking for some 45 minutes, until well after Cass should have been at work. "If you don't stay away from my wife," I finally warned, "you're going to destroy both of our families."

"I'm really sorry, bro," my friend apologized.

But that afternoon I checked my wife's timecard at the denominational headquarters where she worked. She clocked in 59 minutes late, and I realized that it was over. While I hung on to the hope that God might save the marriage, no more offers of hope came from Cass. She was now adamant that she would divorce me and marry Oswardo.

Cass soon moved into another apartment. Oswardo, kicked out of the house by Estelle as long as he kept sleeping with Cass, abandoned his wife and children to move in with her. I could not muster anger against Cass except when I thought of what was happening to Estelle and Oswardo's three precious little children. That was the one element of pain that was too unjust to bear. Once when I saw Estelle and her children, the middle one, a girl of about six, asked me, "Are you going to be our daddy now?"

"It doesn't work like that," Estelle explained to her.

For the first few months of this ordeal, I kept my heart full of the fruit of the Spirit, always loving and forgiving Oswardo.

Eventually, however, my peaceful approach began to give way to anger. ("It's about time," Henry said.) But while Jesus told us to pray for our enemies, He did not mean the way I began doing it. One night I prayed for Oswardo—that God would kill him.

Suddenly God's Spirit reproved my hatred.

I exploded, exasperated. "God, that's not fair! I turned down paying jobs in large churches because I believed You wanted me to lead that small congregation. I've never so much as kissed any woman other than Cass. The only two things I've asked of You are that I could fulfill what You called me to do and that You'd give me a wife so I wouldn't have to be alone. Now You've taken both of them from me. And You're telling me that I can't even hate the man who destroyed all that matters to me!"

In the Bible, God tested everybody He called—Abraham, Sarah, Joseph, Daniel, for example—so I had sometimes wondered what my test would be. Now it was pretty obvious. I was sure, however, that I could not endure mine as those heroes in the Bible did. I did not understand that they, like us, were just ordinary people who did what they had to do. The Bible says that the prophet Elijah, the apostle Paul and others had the same kinds of feelings that we do (see Acts 14:15; James 5:17). The Lord Himself is the Bible's only real hero.

"God, if this is Your test for me," I gasped brokenly, hesitantly, "then I have to confess to You that I can't pass it. I've lived for Your calling. . . . But if this is the price"—it was hard to say, but better to give up a battle I could not survive—"then please give my calling to someone else, and send Cass back tomorrow. I can't endure this pain any longer."

A moment of deep silence followed. For weeks I had mostly been too numb to hear God's voice. Now, however, it pierced the silence. *My child,* He admonished, *Elijah was like you. When Jezebel threatened him, he cried, "God, just let me die." My child, David was like you. When Saul was pursuing him, David almost snapped. He would have killed Nabal if I hadn't used Abigail to stop him. My child, Jeremiah was like you. When others persecuted him, he cried, "Cursed be the day I was born!"*

My child, He continued, *you're a man of God not because of what you are made out of.* That was good, as I was quickly learning. *You're a man of God because I called you, and My grace is enough for you.*

I tried to hold on to those words, to believe that this trial would not be fatal. Could I believe that this one lesson would be worth all the pain—the lesson that God is the real hero, and that when everything else in life is said and done, the story behind our lives is most of all His faithfulness?

In the meantime, I kept matters quiet so that Cass would not feel ashamed to return to me.

So I was surprised when Debbie, a worship leader in the congregation that I had previously pastored, called and asked me point-blank: "Are Cass and Oswardo committing adultery together?"

I was shocked. How did she know? "I can't answer your question," I replied, unwilling to shame my wife, yet also unwilling to lie.

My refusal to answer was confirmation enough, however, and Debbie broke down and wept. "Then it's true," she said. "God woke me up three nights ago, wailing that Cass and Oswardo had rejected His cross, saying they were in adultery. I haven't been able to eat or sleep for three days since I heard it."

Debbie had not been in contact with us for months, but she sent Cass a note calling her to turn back to following God.

I took this as God's assurance that everything would be all right. Surely it meant that Cass would return! I loved my wife; moreover, in the circles I knew, there was no future for me in ministry if I was divorced, regardless of the reason. If God was to fulfill His promises in my life, I assumed Cass *had* to come back.

Brokenness

A by-product of my pain was the fact that I now had no confidence about my ability to hear God. Before Cass left, I had usually prayed for about two hours a day; now I could only mutter Jesus' name over and over. I had always wondered if I would revert to atheism if my faith were shattered. Now I found that where I expected only darkness, God was still there. I could not earn His presence, but He showed Himself beyond my faith.

Although I had always tried to be strong for others, I was now so broken that I needed to be in the presence of the few friends who knew of my pain. I did not need them to talk with me; I just needed to feel the strength of another human being's will to live.

As months passed, sometimes I felt too numb to care whether I lived or died. I knew from my minimal counseling training that when the numbness of trauma begins to wear off, the pain becomes more intense.

One of the leaders in the little congregation I used to pastor called me one day. "Just in case you ever think of suicide," she warned, "remember that hell is much worse than any pain you're experiencing now."

"I don't think that suicide guarantees hell," I protested.

"Are you willing to take that chance?" she pressed. Take a chance on pain worse than what I felt now? Though I did not agree with her theology, I thanked her for caring.

The Impossible Choice

Although Duke University had accepted me into its Ph.D. program in religion, it now seemed meaningless. Indeed, it was financially impossible. My freelance editing work was ending, and the week that Cass left the apartment, she took all our money except the ten dollars I had in my pocket.

I bought nine dollars' worth of groceries; now I had one dollar to my name. The next week I faced a new challenge. Cass and I were sponsoring a child in India for fifteen dollars a month. The money was due. I had a dollar, and was nearly out of groceries again. I prayed desperately, yet without much faith. I still had not told people about the situation, hoping it would help Cass not to be ashamed to return to me.

Late that night, as I was preparing to sleep, a knock came at the door. The person standing there announced that the Lord had led him to give me $25. I almost cried. I had read about such provision happening in the lives of people with great faith. I had no great faith, but I had a great Father who met me at the moment of my need. The next morning I sent off the fifteen dollars for the child in India and bought more groceries.

Each week God provided by one means or another, but I had given up any thought of pursuing my Ph.D.; I just wanted my wife back. Getting her back seemed hopeless, however, in the same city with Oswardo. A psychologist friend encouraged me to continue with school. "Besides, if the relationship between Cass and Oswardo falls apart," he advised, "she'd rather come back to a doctoral student with a future than to an unemployed man without one."

Eventually the choice was presented more starkly: If I stayed put I would soon be living on the street, like people I had served at the Mission. I did not have enough income to pay rent. Meanwhile, the day before I was going to call and turn down my acceptance into the Ph.D. program, my mother phoned to say how happy she was that I would be attending Duke.

"Uh, I guess I'm not going," I said.

"Why not?" she asked, dismayed.

I had not told her that Cass had left. Still, I did not want to lie. "Cass really doesn't want to go," I offered diplomatically.

"But I thought she *wanted* you to do doctoral work." My mother was understandably confused.

"Well," I said, changing the subject slightly, "we really don't have the money to go."

What happened next was completely unexpected. Cass and I had scraped our way through my seminary and her schooling on our own. I did not even know that my mother could afford to pay for such an elite school as Duke. Then she said, "I'll cover the cost if you'll go."

What a commitment of love! Had her call come one day later, I would never have done doctoral work. When I talked with my friends about accepting the money, they said I should recognize it as God's provision.

Meanwhile Cass continued to refuse contact with me. I had been sending notes to her through a common friend, but someone finally disclosed her location to me. The day before I was scheduled to leave town for North Carolina, I visited her. I was hoping for a miracle and ready to change my plans.

"I wish you hadn't come," she said firmly. "It would be easier on you to just let go of me."

I pleaded for reconciliation.

"I'm not coming back no matter what, Craig. You need to let go. The only communication I'll accept from you is business—by which I mean about divorce."

I tried to restrain my tears. She had already told me that she despised my weakness when I wept before her. But the dam inside me burst, and I choked on my tears. The very sight of her ravaged my heart; she appeared to me altogether beautiful, as she always had. For me, the initial spark of romance had only grown over the years.

That was the last day I ever saw this woman that I loved with all my heart. Nothing could totally extinguish that love, though someday I would have to surrender its hope as futile.

I did not think I would ever dare to trust again.

5

Starting Over

Craig

When I arrived in Durham, North Carolina, late on a Saturday afternoon in August, I checked into a cheap motel and asked the clerk about the one-story brick apartment complex across the street. "Don't go over there," she said casually. "There're black people over there, and they'll kill you."

I was stunned by her overt racism. Still, I wanted to be out of my misery, and it would not be considered suicide if it was not my fault. So just in case, I strolled around the apartment buildings in the dark. No one else was outside.

The Projects

I had written to a church in Durham, hoping to connect, but had not heard back. So I called from the motel phone and asked if someone could pick me up for church the next morning. "We don't have any room in the van," the pastor apologized. So the next morning I walked over to the apartments hoping to see someone getting ready for church. Immediately I spotted three well-dressed African American girls chatting near a station wagon.

"Are you heading somewhere?" I inquired hopefully.

"We're getting ready for church," they answered politely. I learned later that they thought perhaps I was a drug dealer.

"Can you tell me about these apartments?" I asked. I could not afford to stay in the motel long.

"You need to ask our grandma," one said. The girls led me into their dark living room and introduced me to their stout grandmother, Josephine Johnson. At first she struck me as stern, but I discovered that she was actually a very strong person shouldering a lot of responsibility.

"That's a good book," I noted, seeing the Bible on the table.

"Yes, it is," she replied. Then she told the three girls along with two others, all of whom ranged in age, I guessed, from seven to thirteen, to go on out to the station wagon. I kept hoping they would invite me to church; I felt it would be rude for me to ask, especially since the car must already be full.

So I returned to the motel and phoned Henry.

"Henry, I'm coming back." I had been there for many hours and had not yet found Christian fellowship.

"You stay there or I'm going to kick your butt," Henry insisted.

So I strolled around Durham examining the exterior of apartment buildings, since the offices were closed on Sunday. I bought no food because I had no idea how long it would take me to find an apartment, and I had very little money.

That afternoon I returned to the motel sunburned and famished. The Johnsons returned from church at the same time. One of the girls called out to me, "Grandma wants to talk with you."

As I stepped into her apartment Grandma Johnson spoke to me. "The Lord told me to offer you somethin' to eat and to invite you to church this mornin'. I didn't obey Him then, but I'm gonna do it now." That was my happy introduction to Southern cooking—three platefuls, in fact. Grandma Johnson and her granddaughters seemed entertained by my appetite.

That evening I attended their service, the only man without a tie. (Friends could not ship my clothes until I had an address, and I owned only a clip-on anyway.) Instead of preaching, the guest evangelist felt led to play a game.

"We'll read verses randomly from the Bible to see if anyone can guess where they are," he said.

This happens to be my favorite game, so I kept whispering the answers to the people around me. Finally, when I gave one answer from Daniel chapter four, the ministers, observing from their position up front what was happening, insisted that I come forward and give my testimony. From that evening on, I was a regular part of the Johnson family.

Having found friendly neighbors, I hoped to move into their complex, into an apartment that Anthony, a Nigerian resident there, told me was available. Though it was getting late, I was able to locate Charlie, the manager. "Come back at nine tomorrow morning," he said. So Monday morning at nine I knocked on his door. "I'm sorry, but no apartments are available here," he informed me.

I staggered away speechless. For some reason this minor rejection, added to my previous months of pain, seemed the final straw. I am ashamed at what transpired over the next few seconds because it is the closest I have ever come to deliberately walking away from God since having known Him.

"God, I've been living for You with all my heart. Now I'm in a strange city, while my wife is somewhere else sleeping with her best friend's husband. God, just to show You how mad I am, I'm going to backslide, just like Cass! Not for very long—just for a couple days. I won't risk dishonoring Your name among people who know I'm Your servant. But I just want to show You how mad I am. Then I'll go back to Missouri and behave myself."

Suddenly the events of the previous night flooded my memory. Those five precious children now looked up to me as a spiritual role model. If I sinned, it could damage their faith.

"God, that was sneaky!" I complained. "I've been here fewer than 48 hours, and already Your honor is at stake." Now I regretted my moment of despair and apologized to the Lord.

Just as abruptly I remembered that Anthony had also told me to come by his place at nine. I always kept my word, a virtue I had learned from my father's integrity, so I knocked. Anthony answered groggily.

"The manager says there are no apartments available," I informed him.

"He's just the manager," Anthony remarked with a wave of his hand, and took me to meet the Realtor instead. By noon I was Anthony's neighbor, and we quickly became friends.

After this I often visited churches with the Johnsons, until they relocated. At first, in my calculating, academic way, I observed how cathartic the joyful services were, given the difficult circumstances in which the members lived. Yet I gradually began to admit how much I needed the catharsis myself.

On my fourth evening in Durham, as I was sitting in the back of a different church quietly contemplating such matters, the pastor summoned me forward. We had never met. She knew nothing about me except that I was the only white person present, that I was not fully participating and that I was not wearing a tie.

"The Lord is going to elevate you, young man," Pastor Weaver prophesied. She reiterated the point a few times. "God will accomplish this no matter what the devil is doing to you right now." Over the next few years, other people who did not know me prophesied the same message to me.

My times with the Johnson family began to reveal to me a world I had never considered. Within my earlier interracial friendships, I had imagined it racist even to notice cultural differences. But now I heard these children chatting about famous African Americans such as Sojourner Truth, whom I had never heard of. They talked about how they took care of their hair and the wonderful food they loved. I considered myself educated, but I began to realize that my strictly white upbringing had left me utterly ignorant of how a significant part of my own country lives—how my own brothers and sisters in Christ live.

More importantly, I noticed how these children endured a setting so different from the one I had grown up in. Church people seemed to provide youth in this neighborhood the only alternative role model to drugs and casual sex. Because the various mothers of these five children were on drugs, their grandmother was raising them by herself.

Yet these children handled their hardships far better than I was handling my grief. Further I found that their church welcomed me in a way that most white churches did not—indeed, in some white churches my marital status made me a pariah, a moral leper. The white churches I knew had many resources, but the black church over the centuries had learned how to deal with pain.

Right then, that was the gift I needed most.

Grieving and Learning

I passed through different stages of grief. Sometimes I felt guilty, contemplating every disagreement Cass and I had ever had, though usually we had ended those by making up tearfully.

Other times I felt desperate to be worthy of her love, yet despaired of achieving it. I remembered the reasons she had given for preferring Oswardo to me and felt ugly, awkward and useless. Cass would not have wanted me to feel that way; those were fleeting excuses, the words of a moment.

Meanwhile only God protected me from the temptations that burned in my heart. I knew that if God ever chose to use me, it would be wholly because He was gracious. I still shared Christ with people, but differently now than before. I shared with them Good News as a fellow human being who needed and experienced God's mercy.

And God in His grace worked through me. Some of the students whom I led to Christ and mentored have now led far more people to Christ than I. Some had me baptize them in campus swimming pools. A couple of science graduate students I mentored quickly became my peers. Some students received powerful experiences with the Spirit as I prayed with them or shared what I felt God was saying to them.

Eventually I sometimes shared with students the lessons I learned from being abandoned. One time a student insisted, "I can't believe in a God who would punish people for sin."

"God disciplines us to deter us from the greatest punishment of all—being alienated from Him forever," I explained, offering relevant passages from the Bible.

"It's *especially* hell I don't believe in," she retorted. "And if you persuade me that there's such a place as hell, then I just won't believe in God at all!"

Simply quoting verses to my young friend was not going to accomplish much, so I asked if I could tell her a story.

"Go ahead," she agreed.

I told about the breakup of my marriage and how painful it was that my wife had left me.

"As long as I feel hope that my wife might return," I said, "I can endure the pain of her rejecting me. But on the days that I cannot muster that hope, the pain feels unendurable, and I just want to give up fighting the divorce." I paused and could see that the student was listening sympathetically.

"In the same way," I suggested, "a God of infinite love has infinite pain over our rejection of Him—so great that He chose to endure the pain of the cross rather than the pain of our rejection. So if we still keep rejecting His love for us day after day, eventually the time comes when God declares, 'I grant you the divorce.' If we abandon Him," I concluded, "it's not God's love but ours that failed."

Rejection from Christians

Spiritual support helped me survive. Many people from the rural, interdenominational church I had joined in Missouri were supportive. I found support also in North Carolina, and not just from African American Christians and campus ministries. One night, for example, I wandered into the midweek Bible study at a local Presbyterian church. The associate pastor was teaching through the books of the Bible, and that night he happened to be teaching from the book of Hosea.

"Hosea had to experience betrayal so God's people could see what they were doing to God," he explained.

I began to wonder: If I was learning the lesson of Hosea, then would God send my wife back to me—as He had restored Hosea's wife? But the minister warned me afterward that God works in different ways at different times.

What eventually stung most deeply was the rejection of some fellow Christians who learned of our separation and condemned me, keeping the wounds fresh. Jesus defended people from being divorced unjustly, but some Christians have twisted His teaching to abuse those He defended. People who knew neither my wife nor me charged: "She wouldn't have left you for nothing."

"What about Hosea?" I tried to protest. "Or God, whose people often proved unfaithful to Him?"

"If God hadn't made Himself so unapproachably holy," one Christian retorted, "Israel wouldn't have felt so alienated from Him."

In other words, those Christians had decided that, one way or another, if I had done something differently my wife would not have been unfaithful. I felt that placated my accusers with the assurance that no such tragedy would ever befall them. Was I a worse husband than others, simply because my spouse was unfaithful and theirs were not?

"This is like punishing a rape victim to prove you're against rape!" I pleaded, but my protests fell on deaf ears.

One couple in another state who knew Cass and me heard about our separation and wrote to me. "We're breaking fellowship with you until you repent from being separated from your wife," they declared. "This is God's judgment on you for pursuing higher education. Now you'll be alone for the rest of your life."

Many people have false stereotypes of ultra-conservative Christians, but unfortunately some Christians do fit that mold.

I joined the InterVarsity campus minister's Pentecostal church. Especially since my early lessons in hearing God's voice, I had often experienced the spiritual gift called prophecy, speaking what one hears God saying. This gift is quite prominent throughout the Bible and is part of the experience of hundreds of millions of Christians today. At its worst it can be inaccurate or abused, but in its mature form it can be very helpful.

In this Pentecostal church, God gave me prophecies almost every week. Sometimes the prophecies quoted the very texts of Scripture or gave the same message that, unknown to me, the pastor was going to preach about that day. Although the pastor insisted initially that it takes two to break up a marriage, in time he understood that I really was serving the Lord. The denomination, however, could not waive its policy against ordaining ministers whose spouses left them if the ministers ever remarried.

I resolved to embrace my shame, humbling myself under the Lord's hand and letting Him exalt me in due time—if it pleased Him. I recalled from being physically beaten on various occasions that sometimes if one stays down long enough, the beater gets bored or tired and goes away. "Let the enemy curse," David once said. "Perhaps the Lord will have compassion on my suffering and grant me blessing instead of his cursing this day" (2 Samuel 16:11–12).

The Reminder

The rejections forced me to remember that it was God who had called me, and only God could fulfill my calling. It was hard to believe that He would ever use me in any way except one on one with the individuals He would bring to me. Yet despite my own lack of strength to believe, His call kept burning inside me; I could not escape it. Perhaps all I could do for this world's suffering was make a dent, but I would make as big a dent as I could.

Cass had made choices, true, but God was allowing me to go through that pain for a reason. My pain could help me feel a loving God's broken heart for the world's pain. I had learned earlier to hear God through the Spirit in prayer and through careful study of the Bible; now I learned to hear Him in a new way. To care about what God cares about is to feel His heart.

6

The Encounter

Craig

Cass finally secured the divorce on the grounds that we had not
lived together for over two years. As soon as the news came, I
knelt and read the words of 1 Corinthians 7:15 one more time:
"The brother or sister is not bound to the marriage in these
circumstances." I knew from ancient divorce contracts that *not
bound* was how Paul's contemporaries declared a person free
from his or her former marriage, hence able to remarry.

Now, for the first time since Cass had left, I tried to remove
my wedding ring. My flesh was tight around it. As I continued
to wrestle with it, it maneuvered off slowly, painfully—the final,
excruciating symbol of the tragic rending of one flesh. Marriage
was never meant to be broken.

Despite the sorrow, I suddenly felt the Spirit overwhelm me
in a profound way. God reiterated what I had heard from Him
shortly before I had moved to North Carolina. *You see, My
child, you are a man of God not because of what you are made*

of, but because I called you. Now you've discovered that you were even weaker than you thought. Yet when the temptations became too great for you, I always removed them or gave you new strength to endure them. Now, My child, you understand that you are a man of God—not because of who you are, but because of who I am.

To encounter God's grace so deeply was worth all the pain.

A Beautiful Woman from Congo

Because I had trusted Cass so completely, I was now desperately afraid to enter any new relationship. I was also fairly sure that no one would ever be interested in me. Nevertheless I started praying for a wife, determined to be as faithful to her in advance as I had been to my first wife. The two things I knew beyond any doubt were God's faithfulness and my calling to preach and teach the Gospel. God showed me that, since I knew my calling, I should not consider marrying anyone who rejected it.

At Duke I was helping Joe, the InterVarsity staff worker, disciple students. Joe informed me that one of the new doctoral students who would be attending our meetings was from Congo. A woman named Médine Moussounga had been part of the French-speaking arm of the International Fellowship of Evangelical Students; InterVarsity was the U.S. branch.

A month after my divorce went through, Médine attended a meeting of the fellowship. When I first saw Médine, I was struck by her beauty—her large black eyes, her thick black eyebrows, her brown complexion and slender figure. My second realization was an amazing coincidence. The thought had recently crossed my mind that the ideal partner for me in ministry might be an African whose studies focused on African American history. That happened to be Médine's dissertation focus.

Ministry commitment mattered most, though. And it probably would not work out between us anyway. My confidence was at rock bottom. Thus I tried not to treat her differently from any of my other peers. Still, she was not easy to forget, and I mentioned the matter to the Lord.

Our next group meeting came about a month later. Knowing that Médine was from Congo, I tried a conversational long shot. I mentioned the only other person associated with Congo that I knew—even though I was aware only of his ministry in the other, larger Congo (at that time called Zaire).

"Have you ever heard of a Swiss missionary named Jacques Vernaud?" I ventured.

Médine's eyes seemed to light up. "He was close friends with my father." She laughed. "He started ministry in our Congo before he moved to Zaire. How do you know of him?"

Despite her appearing pleased, the tone of her voice sounded casual, almost offhand. I had a sinking feeling that she was merely amused by my attempt to converse about her vastly different culture.

"I went to college with his daughter," I explained. "As a baby she was healed of leukemia after prayer, and she told us some of Jacques Vernaud's stories." I told Médine that I was impressed by the fact that he stayed secretly in Zaire even when missionaries were being killed. "I got to meet him and his wife when they were visiting their daughters," I added. We chatted further.

The Matter of Tongues

Unfortunately the rest of our evening did not proceed as pleasantly. It was an interdenominational setting in which each participant brought a distinctive contribution. I had chosen to lead the discussion that evening on an area in which my background and experience gave me something special to offer: I shared about praying in tongues.

As I explained my views to the other students, I was careful not to suggest that this is the most important gift from the Holy

Spirit, or that those who pray this way are better Christians than others. Instead I said that I believe tongues offers a valuable dimension of prayer, a way to pray from the depths of the heart beyond what we would normally verbalize.

Everyone appeared enthusiastic to learn more about tongues except two students—of whom one was Médine. But I believed Scripture was clear, so I forged ahead, recounting my first experience with speaking in tongues fourteen years earlier. I told how two days after my conversion, as I entrusted my life more formally to Christ as Lord and Savior, I experienced the same sense of God's awesome majesty I had felt during my conversion. I was so overwhelmed by God's presence that I had to thank Him, yet I could not praise Him worthily enough unless He gave me the best words for that—and of course God knows lots of languages! As I worshiped, the words came out in a language I did not know. I had never heard of this experience and did not know that there was a name for it.

"At that first experience," I said, "I worshiped in tongues for perhaps an hour or two, shuddering with deep, cathartic laughter while my academically oriented brain tried to scrutinize the grammar of the new language. When I finished I felt somehow different.

"For years up to that point I had tried to discover meaning in life analytically," I added, "but during that intense spiritual experience I discovered that I'd found in God the very purpose for which I had been made. I would give God everything that was in me."

When time came for group discussion after my talk, I grew certain that there was no potential for a relationship with Médine. She was outspoken and quick, challenging and contradicting my words. Tongues was a very valuable gift in my life, one that I hoped some other students would want to share. Her firm rejection of it left no possibility of anything more than friendship between us. Worse, I was still very sensitive to conflict, and the last thing I wanted was an argumentative relationship.

Still, I did not want hard feelings between us. A few days after our disastrous public disagreement, I gave her a gift: a T-shirt with a slogan protesting apartheid.

"It's to make up for our disagreement the other day," I said, handing her the shirt. She laughed and let me sit with her, rather nervously, during the lecture we were attending at her church, the Presbyterian church where I had heard the study on Hosea. Afterward I walked her to a nearby grocery store, but she looked so stunningly attractive that I questioned my motives and hurried home.

After this, Médine and my other African friends invited me to their various gatherings. I enjoyed those times, but the cultural differences were significant. One night Médine and her Kenyan friend Mary were finishing preparing fish for dinner, and told the rest of us to go ahead and start eating the food that was hot on the table.

We kept urging Médine and Mary to join us, over their protests. Finally I joked, "They're waiting because the food is poisoned."

Everyone fell instantly silent. I realized that my feeble attempt at humor had failed severely.

"Sorry," I added quickly. "I meant not *poison*, which is French for 'poison,' but *poisson*, which is French for 'fish.'"

Médine was the only one who laughed.

7

The Question of Marriage

Médine

Craig was not the only one looking for God's leading about a future spouse. During my eight months as an exchange student in the United States, I was praying for my future husband and even getting certain ideas about what he might be like. After several of those months, I thought God was telling me that I already knew him, but God would not say who it was.

I had already resolved the question of interracial marriage. While in France, before coming to America, I had watched the movie *Cry Freedom*, which is about apartheid. I had concluded by the movie's end that the barrier between whites and blacks was too great to consider intimate relationships like marriage between them.

But then I began to notice how many of my kind Christian friends were white. Some time later another black friend and I were watching another film that highlighted racism. We kept criticizing whites' insensitivity until we remembered that the Christian friend we had brought, who was sitting nervously between us, was white.

Of all the men I met in the U.S., I was most interested in Craig. Craig was tall and handsome, but he also seemed enigmatic. I could not understand why someone who obviously loved God as much as he did seemed to carry so much pain behind his smile. Why was he so sensitive and insecure?

I wore the T-shirt he gave me. I was surprised and pleased by his thoughtful gift, but I pondered what his words meant when he gave it to me. Yes, we had disagreed, but why was that a problem? Could two people not express opposing sides of an issue?

My experience with tongues was very different from his. I had been in circles where some people treated me as a second-class Christian because I did not speak in tongues. Their disapproval challenged the heart of my identity as a lover of God. Disturbed, I had once asked my father what he thought about it.

"We all have different gifts, Médine," he explained. "Some people have that gift. You and I have different ones." As I mentioned earlier, people were often healed when my father prayed, a gift that started when Jacques Vernaud laid hands on him.

Clearly one did not need to pray in tongues to be spiritual. My family belonged to the mainstream Protestant church in my country, Église Évangelique du Congo, and the church welcomed spiritual gifts because they were in the Bible. Nevertheless I thought many Congolese Pentecostals I met were eccentric. I hoped that Craig was not like those people who insisted that everyone had to pray in tongues to be spiritual.

The vocal expression I enjoyed in public debate, however, was not matched in matters of the heart. In my culture women often acted uninterested even when they were interested, depending on the man to initiate.

So one evening when Craig called me, simply to chat, I responded as any woman I knew from back home would respond. After a few words of greeting, I laughed. "Nice to talk with you, brother. Okay, I'd better get back to my homework now."

After this, Craig did not call much. I could only assume that he was not interested in me.

Thus, when my time in the U.S. as an exchange student ended and I returned to my studies in France, I was open when Christophe, a French white convert in my church who was intensely devoted to Christ, wanted to spend time with me. Christophe was a humble and zealous man of God. *Maybe he's the future husband the Lord said I already know,* I thought.

Craig

Even after Médine left the U.S., her name kept coming up— especially when I shared with some students about the love of Jesus. "Médine Moussounga told me the same thing," one student noted when I shared the Gospel with him. To me Médine had been the most impressive witness on campus.

Médine was also gifted and attractive. I could not imagine that someone like her could ever have any interest in me— especially given our apparent theological differences. Plus, along with my shyness, I was inhibited by the concerns of feminist friends about men overstepping their bounds. And besides, when I had worked up my courage and called her that evening after giving her the T-shirt, hoping to strike up a conversation, I had gotten my answer. She had hurried to get off the phone. Obviously she was not interested in me, so I did not try again. I continued to respect her but knew that we would not become involved romantically.

An African male friend did try to explain to me that African women act disinterested *especially* when they are interested.

"So how do you know when an African woman is interested in you?" I asked, confused. "It seems they'll act disinterested either way."

"That's a problem," he acknowledged.

One day when Médine's African friends on campus were looking at pictures taken at one of our earlier meetings, I was struck again by Médine's beauty and kicked myself. Here was someone godly, brilliant and beautiful. What was I looking for, anyway? As the evening broke up I asked her friend Mary for Médine's address.

"I can give you her address," Mary said, but then warned quietly, "but I believe she is seeing someone in France."

My heart sank. Obviously someone as wonderful as Médine would be dating someone. Nevertheless I wrote to her as friends, and she and I became faithful correspondents.

After a few awkward attempts at other relationships, I resolved not to date anyone until I found the person I would marry.

Médine

That summer I visited Congo. A man of prayer told my father this: "Médine is going to work for the Lord, but outside the country." In a violation of tradition, he added, "She will also marry someone not descended from her father's people."

Even more explicitly, Mama Suzanne, a family friend, told me this: "I feel that God is saying that you will marry a white man someday."

"Oh! That must be Christophe, my friend in France!" I exclaimed.

"No, not this white man," Suzanne prophesied, "but a different one."

Now I was confused. Prophecies must be tested, and perhaps this one was wrong. But after I returned to France from Congo, Christophe asked to speak to me.

"Médine," he apologized, "you are very special to me, but when I pray, I don't feel that it's God's will for us to pursue the relationship."

He broke off our relationship, and I felt devastated.

8

In Black and White

Médine was one of many international friends from outside my culture, but I found myself most comfortable in the African American community. The day that Grandma Johnson heard God tell her to feed me and take me to church, she could not have known the long-range effect on my life. The neighborhood where I settled initially and the welcome I received in African American churches made me feel at home.

Arthur Williams was starting an African American Bible study group at Duke and invited me to help out because of my Bible knowledge. One night many of the young men in the study group were watching the movie *Cry Freedom*. As the anti-white sentiment in the room grew, I began feeling more and more conspicuous, but everyone treated me as just part of the group. That was when I discovered that anger against racism did not usually translate into hostility toward white friends.

Being in the group also exposed me to conversations I would not have heard otherwise. "That student called me a n—," one of my trusted friends told me one day. As if assuming I already knew, others chimed in about incidents of racism that they had experienced that week, some even laughing casually about it as if this were life as normal.

This was shocking to me. How could people treat my friends like this? And how could it be going on daily while I, their own brother in Christ, remained oblivious to it? Though I had been too polite to say it, I had long assumed that the civil rights movement had mostly resolved the *real* racism, except for a few crazy white supremacists.

After the others had dispersed, I lingered. "Arthur—those incidents that our friends were mentioning—those kinds of things don't happen often, do they?"

Arthur eyed me sadly. "The first day of my first English class at Duke," he recounted, "I was the only African American in the room. The professor called me aside after class. 'You need to drop this class,' she told me, 'and if you tell anyone I said this, it'll be your word against mine.'"

I was horrified. I had doubted the reality of racism because I had never experienced it—but then, I *would not* have experienced it. Meanwhile whites so outnumbered blacks that if even just a handful were overtly racist, African Americans would be confronted with racism regularly. I began to remember some white friends' offhand comments that I had previously just dismissed uncomfortably.

Through the patience of Arthur and others, I began to cross a cultural line over which I could not return without deliberately pretending that I knew no better. I also began to feel suspicion directed toward me as I came to the other side of the line. My black friends accepted me, but with every new black community or individual who did not know me, I felt I had to "prove" myself all over again.

I always persevered; the longest someone held my love at bay was a year. But the proving was painful—giving me just a taste of what my African American friends experience regularly in a predominantly white world.

The Black Church

I felt increasingly certain that God was leading me to stop simply appreciating interracial ministry; I was supposed to join an African American church. But which one?

One day an attractive African American friend named Kecia invited me to visit Orange Grove Baptist Church with her. Kecia never went back after that night, but I felt drawn to the church. Carl, the pastor, had no one else who could pick up visitors, so he picked me up himself. On the way to church he shared with me his vision. "Some churches just want to reach the middle class," he said, "but we want to reach drug addicts, prostitutes and people that a lot of other churches don't want." I remembered the neighborhood where I had lived when I first moved to Durham.

Like me, Carl was also looking for a friend. As time passed our common vision and friendship eventually convinced me to join the church. "But I prophesy every week in church," I warned him.

Carl hesitated. "Well, that's probably never happened here before," he observed. "But it's in the Bible, so if the Spirit moves you to do it, you've got to do it." With my previous church's public blessing I joined Orange Grove, and Carl brought me on as an associate minister. Arthur helped me with the biggest logistical transition: He taught me how to tie a tie. There. Becoming a Baptist was not so very complicated!

In one student Bible study, after Carl shared about ethnic reconciliation, I prophesied. As the Lord wept that His Body was divided by race, I could almost feel pain tearing me in half, the pain of Christ's Body that should not be divided. Meanwhile the Spirit never once moved me to prophesy at the Baptist church. Carl made space for me to teach during the service, however, and I was able to let the Spirit guide me in how to do that; occasionally that teaching included discussion of spiritual gifts, and some members began to catch that vision. Carl also welcomed me to start a ministry to college students; eventually about fifty students attended the church.

Carl had learned a great deal from the Nation of Islam before his conversion. He advised me to read *The Autobiography of Malcolm X*, *The Slave Narratives* and some fairly radical Afrocentric works. As I kept reading I was appalled at what people who looked like me had done to people who looked like my closest friends. I became so ashamed of the color of my skin that I felt like taking a knife and peeling it off, but as Carl preached each week how God made all of us in His image, I understood that I, too, was made in God's image.

I also wept as I realized what it had meant for the gracious people of Orange Grove to embrace me. Some of them had lived through the civil rights movement. Some had suffered from whites while participating in "sit-ins." Some older members had even known people born into slavery. And yet—they loved me as a brother in Christ, regardless of my skin color.

I was ordained at Orange Grove soon after I received my doctorate. The association sent an older minister to offer the ministerial charge, and she began praying over me in tongues.

"If you stay humble," she prophesied, "God says He will use you."

Carl, who had chosen a journalism major in college, did not know of any white ministers in recent history ordained in the

National Baptist Convention, at least in the South. Unknown to me, he had an extra opportunity in mind. To my surprise, local television covered my ordination, and the Associated Press and Religious News Service soon carried stories on it as well. One Atlanta newspaper carried a two-page story. Many of the accounts mentioned my earlier conversion from atheism. For years I had shared my testimony with people one on one. Now when I was not even trying to share it, it went out to tens of thousands of people all at once!

The Commentary

I had easily invested more than ten thousand hours in research on Bible background, always intending to make the information available to the Church if no one else did that first. It seemed unreasonable to expect ordinary pastors or students to research for ten thousand hours before beginning to preach! I kept my research on some hundred thousand index cards, hoping to put the background for each passage at readers' fingertips.

Because I was involved with InterVarsity at Duke, I considered proposing my idea to InterVarsity Press. I had not yet done so when an editor from that publisher read one of my articles and called me, asking if I would be interested in submitting something for publication.

I proposed the background commentary, but life quickly distracted me: I could not find a teaching position. Surely God would not provide twelve years of college study for me and then leave me unable to find a position. Time was rapidly running out. I tried to have faith, but by July it was obvious that I would not have a teaching position for the fall.

One Sunday evening I figured out how much I would need to live on that year, to keep both my research files and myself from becoming homeless. I despaired at the figure.

The next day the editor called. "We want you to write the background commentary."

"Thanks, Rodney," I acknowledged, trying to muster enthusiasm.

Meanwhile I was thinking, *How am I going to write this book while living on the street?*

"And," he added, "we want to offer you an advance."

The figure he mentioned matched to the dollar the amount that I had computed the night before.

Toward the end of my time at Duke, a Latina sister named Neyda gave me a prophecy. "God earlier promised to exalt you. The exaltation is now about to begin."

"I'm afraid," I protested. "I might become proud and then God will have to bring me down again."

Neyda smiled. "That won't be necessary," she explained. "You know enough to stay down this time."

9

Just Friends

Craig

A few years had now passed since Médine and I had seen each other, although we stayed in touch by mail. In the process of our correspondence, I tried to comfort Médine regarding her singleness.

In one letter I assured her that she was everything a man could want. I even admitted that I had fond feelings for her. Then to make sure that I was not causing any misunderstanding, I added, "But I don't think God intends for us to be more than friends." I explained that my calling ruled out marrying someone who did not share my heart to pour one's entire life into ministry. I had already been married once to someone who, even despite initially professing a call to ministry, ultimately showed little vision for sacrificing to serve the needs of the world. I was not willing to risk marrying someone who did not share the kind of sacrificial calling I saw with Paul's companions in the Bible or with the early movement of Wesley or others. Nobody without that vision could feel comfortable with me or my heart.

Médine

As Craig and I corresponded and occasionally phoned after I returned to France, I admitted to him that he was my best friend.

I had, however, also begun to feel something more. I liked Craig increasingly and even daydreamed about him. I could confide in him the same way I could confide in my older brother, Emmanuel. But there was one matter about which I could not confide in him: I had begun to feel as though the Lord was saying that *Craig* was the husband He had spoken to me about.

I penned a delicately worded letter to Craig, admitting that I was not called to ministry. That is, I was not called to be a pastor. But perhaps Craig meant *ministry* more broadly?

Craig

In her return letter, Médine affirmed my concern that she was not called to ministry; she was just an "ordinary" person.

Had I read her vitally important, middle-of-the-letter description of what she considered an "ordinary" person to be, I would have seen that these were the very qualities I longed for in a wife. She had helped start a church and was on its leadership team. She was working with drug addicts and evangelizing among the poor, among college students and among immigrants in France. Sometimes she even did open-air preaching.

But her opening lines had arrested my attention, and I thought I could see where it was headed. "You noted that you don't think God intends us to be more than friends," Médine's letter began. "Are you sure about that?"

In my haste to read her conclusion about our "friendship," I skipped swiftly to the end. There I read Médine's confession of her long-term feelings for me and her acknowledgment that she had been waiting for me to broach the issue.

As I realized her interest in me, my emotions began to run wild for her. But I also felt an immediate check in my heart. Did Médine have the strength to endure marriage to me, especially considering my rigorous calling? And the spiritual gift of tongues seemed too central to my prayer life for me to marry someone who opposed it. Moreover I wanted to spend the rest of my life in the African American community, a culture very different from Médine's own.

Most important, I had to be honest with myself; her words were emblazoned there on the paper before me. Médine said explicitly that she was not called to ministry. I decided I had better tame my heart and stem her romantic interest in me before it went further, before our feelings overwhelmed our common sense. I had suffered pain, and the last thing I wanted to do was lead someone on—all the more if it was someone for whom I felt such deep affection. That caution had long protected me from wrong relationships.

I wrote back immediately, knowing that Médine would be awaiting a reply. "I feel the same way about you," I explained, "but I doubt that our callings are compatible."

But then I added a few cautious words: "If you feel that I'm mistaken about that, let's discuss it further." Biased by my feelings, I harbored a little hope that she might persuade me to think differently.

Her returning letter sank that hope. "Your concern is right, brother," she wrote, "so we'll just be friends."

Médine

Brokenhearted by Craig's letter, I buried my feelings, unwilling to risk sharing them again. I continued to love Craig, but

I concluded that ours was an impossible love. I could not tell him all the tears that had gone into my reply, acknowledging that we would just be friends.

Craig

Every time I listened to Médine's joyful, Spirit-filled faith in her letters I wondered if I had closed the matter prematurely. But I could not risk hurting her. In the very unlikely event that God wanted us together He could make that clear, but I now had little expectation that He would do so.

The matter settled, I somehow never went back to read the middle of her letter. It would be seven long years before I realized my dreadful oversight.

10

Drug Dealers
and White Supremacists

Craig

By this time I was teaching in another part of North Carolina at a seminary within an African American Methodist denomination. My apartment was across the street from the adjoining college, where I also helped with the campus ministry and campus church. I was now living and working in the African American community and rarely went outside it for the first three of my four years there.

Despite the many considerate white people in town, I learned of more incidents of racism than I have room to narrate in this book. It was no surprise to me that a former imperial wizard of the Ku Klux Klan lived just outside of town. One of my colleagues was paranoid, but if racists had burned a cross on my lawn I would have been paranoid, too.

A more immediate issue in my own neighborhood was the drug dealers. "When drug dealers stray into the white section of town," my neighbors complained, "the police chase them back into our section." This strategy was called "containment." I was probably one of the few men in the neighborhood who did not own a gun for protection, but I never advertised that deficiency.

Some of my neighbors watched out for me, especially Julia, a kind older lady next door. Occasionally I learned of murders, at least one on the street right behind me. Much more regularly, drug dealers worked in broad daylight; indeed, sometimes I had to excuse myself to get past the drug dealers I would find sitting on my front porch.

In my spare time I told Bible stories to neighborhood children. Some of them were afraid of the drug dealers, who apparently did not appreciate my activities. "They told us to stay away from you," two children reported to me dutifully, "but we told them we wouldn't because Mr. Craig is our friend."

"Thanks," I offered, wincing. Wanting my scholarship to serve the Church, I hoped to avoid expiring prematurely.

Though my toes often protruded from my shoes—I was trying to live simply—I bought shoes for two of the children. Some parents welcomed me, but one boy's mother did not believe initially that I was a preacher. Unlike usual preachers, I wore blue jeans and did not drive a nice (or any) car. One Sunday I visited her church, and her pastor prophesied publicly that God was going to use me greatly. The mother liked me after that.

Drug dealers were another story. One day a car of the kind we expected drug dealers to drive followed several children and me very closely as I walked them home from a Christian concert. The boy suggested, "If they follow us a few more feet, I'll dart over there to my aunt's house. You keep them busy."

"Okay," I agreed uncomfortably, praying steadily under my breath. Happily for us, the car moved on.

With the drug dealers also came drug addicts, some of whom I got to know. My heart especially went out to the mother of one of the children I told Bible stories to. Her beauty, in fact, reminded me of Médine. Her condition tore my heart apart— had circumstances been different, I wondered . . .

With drug addicts came drug crime. One warm day I returned from class after having left my back window open for an hour. I heard an ominous clatter inside as I opened the door. Annoyed, I strode around to the back of the building in time to find a gaunt-looking man dropping hastily from my window. He had cut my screen and climbed through the window.

"Come here, sir!" I demanded, too angry to consider what I was doing. "I want to talk with you." Glancing back nervously, he hurried off. We were both the safer for it. For that matter, nothing in my apartment was worth stealing; he had just drunk some orange juice. Aware of my vulnerability, however, it was many nights before I slept peacefully.

Another day I was on the phone with Cecilia, one of my former students from Orange Grove's Sunday school, now a law student at Vanderbilt. Hearing banging on the door, I asked her to wait for a moment and put her on speakerphone. When I opened the door an intoxicated man demanded, "Ted, I want my dollar."

"Sir, I don't owe you any money, and my name isn't Ted." I have no idea how he confused me with someone else; I was the neighborhood's only white resident.

He remained insistent. "I want my dollar, Ted." I gently placed my hand against his chest to move him back from the doorway so I could close the door. He glared first at my hand on his chest, then at my face, and then hurled himself forward in a rage. I found myself pushing the door from one side, while he was shoving from the other. I could not close it because he had jammed his foot in the doorway.

"Craig, what's going on?" Cecilia called through the speaker-phone. Hearing the voice and assuming that someone was with me, my uninvited guest withdrew his foot from the door just long enough for me to slam and bolt it. I never did learn who Ted was.

During my fourth year there, my neighbors observed grate-fully that the police were finally cracking down on drug dealers in our neighborhood. Pleased, I sent the police department a thank-you note. One afternoon, however, as I was jogging, an officer new to the neighborhood pulled over beside me.

"Sir, do you know what kind of neighborhood this is?" he warned. "There are *drug dealers* here."

What news! I thought. My eyes quickly scanned the children playing in nearby yards. He had not warned *them* about the drug dealers. Although his concern for me was understandable, I could not fathom a system that left children less protected. That evening in class I announced to my students, all of whom were African American pastors, that I had finally been pulled over on account of my race. After they finished laughing, each one recounted his own pulling-over experiences.

At the time, the Nation of Islam's claim that Christianity was a "white religion" was proving influential. Glenn Usry, an African American pastor, was one of my students and friends. He had been interested in joining the Nation of Islam before he experienced a revelation from Christ. Together we worked to refute the "white religion" claim, with me doing a lot of the research for our two books together. Glenn and I laughingly took bets on whether the Nation of Islam or the Klan would want to kill us first.

Glenn probably came closest to winning the informal bet. Challenging the spread of the Nation of Islam in an African American area, he began passing out leaflets based on our re-search. One afternoon a Muslim confronted him: "It might be necessary for you to be killed."

Later Glenn mentioned to me, "By the way, I put your name on the tracts. I want to credit you for your research."

"Uh, thanks, Glenn," I gulped.

The most prevalent day-to-day danger, however, and one I less preferred to think about, remained the drug dealers.

Médine

I completed my doctoral program and began making plans to return to Congo, but I confided in Craig that I was anxious because civil war was erupting there. He pleaded with me not to return yet, assuring me that he could help me find a job in the United States, maybe at his school. But he had already shared with me about the dangers in his neighborhood.

"I can see that life even in the U.S. is dangerous," I wrote back. "Wherever we are is in God's hands. So I might as well go home and be with my family."

I could not tell him the primary reason that I was not willing to accept his offer. It would be too painful to be in the same city with him and unable to express my love for him.

We continued to share our hearts in our letters—on every issue except how we felt about each other. That one area was too painful to discuss. Craig and I each spoke assurances that we were praying for the other that God would send a more suitable spouse than ourselves.

11

Conflict at Home

Craig

Even though drug dealers remained my most pressing problem, I now had a new one. My first book with Glenn Usry challenged white racism harshly. After the newspaper announced the book, my water bill doubled. One student I knew from church had worked briefly for city utilities. He told how his coworkers there had exchanged racist jokes and hung a Sambo picture on the wall. When they discovered that the student was gathering documentation to report them, they fired him. So I should not have been surprised that my water bill doubled. The next month it quadrupled, and the next month it quintupled.

"I think there's a leak," I wrote to city utilities.

"You have no leak," they wrote back.

After I finally moved, the water bills dropped to normal. At least no one burned a cross on the lawn.

That town had been a lonely place for me anyway, though I did start making more friends my final year there. By then I was again fasting a day every week to keep close to God, especially to keep my heart pure before Him.

I grew certain that God wanted me to relocate either to Philadelphia or to New York. I was so sure that this was God's direction, I decided to move whether I had a teaching position or not. Thus I wrote to my friend Ron Sider, a renowned Anabaptist ethicist at Eastern Seminary in Philadelphia, that I would be willing to teach there in return for an apartment on campus.

"Interesting," Ron responded. "We have a visiting professorship available this year in biblical studies." It paid just enough to cover the expenses of the missionary-in-residence apartment, which happened to be vacant that year. And Eastern actually had more African American students than the African American seminary where I was teaching.

"I'm coming," I announced.

It was only when I was halfway to Eastern Seminary that my moving date struck me. I had spent almost exactly nine years in North Carolina, and it was seven years to the day since my divorce had gone through. God had placed me among wonderfully caring people in North Carolina to facilitate my healing. Now I felt it was time for me to get back to work full-time for the Lord.

Eastern Seminary (later renamed Palmer Seminary of Eastern University) felt like home even before I got there. Known for its ethnic diversity, it had for years been near the top of my list of places I wanted to teach. Because I would be living on the seminary campus, an additional advantage was that I no longer had to contend with drug dealers on my front porch.

I had once despaired of ever being useful for God's Kingdom and wondered if my life could even be worth living. Over the years, however, God had begun "lifting" me back up in ministry, just as others had predicted. My books, especially the background commentary, were now serving tens of thousands of pastors and scholars in their work.

I was also less lonely in Philadelphia. In addition to the seminary, I found Enon Tabernacle Baptist Church. The pastor, Alyn Waller, was a recent graduate of the seminary's D.Min. program, and he welcomed me as one of the associate ministers.

When I was not teaching, much of my day was spent doing research and writing. During prayer I began getting the sense that God wanted me to write about the book of Revelation for Zondervan. I had never written anything for Zondervan, however, and I was so busy working on another commentary that I never got around to contacting them.

One day a Zondervan editor called. "We have a cancellation in the NIV Application series," Jack informed me. "We were wondering if you'd be interested in contributing."

"I'm really honored that you'd ask," I said, "but I don't know how I'd have time." Nevertheless I ventured, "What book is it on?"

"Revelation," Jack answered.

I shut my eyes. "Uh—I think I'd better say yes."

I grew so content in my work that I almost stopped thinking about a wife. I did not, however, stop praying for Médine. Anxious for her safety, I had sought prayer support before I moved to Eastern from Jackie Reeves, an A.M.E. minister in New Jersey who was a spiritual mentor to me.

"I feel God saying that He's going to protect Médine," Jackie had said, "and also that He'll send her a husband who is a spiritual warrior."

I prayed that God would remove any hindrances to fulfilling both parts of that prophecy.

Meanwhile another spiritual mentor had assured me that the Lord was saying that I already knew my future wife, and that she and I were just too stubborn to see it.

"You're mistaken," I assured him diplomatically.

He shook his head and told me to check a certain month in my journal. Only years later did I realize that that month was when I met Médine.

Médine

Craig wrote to tell me the encouraging words Jackie had spoken, and I felt God's protecting hand from the very start. As I prepared for my flight from France to Brazzaville, the capital and largest city of the Republic of the Congo, I learned to my dismay that I had accidentally booked my flight for the wrong date—a day in the previous month! I had to schedule another flight and felt embarrassed until I learned that the airport in Brazzaville was bombed the very day that I had meant to fly.

I suddenly remembered the vision that Coco Moïse had received when I was five years old. He had seen me returning to the airport from a distant country; then he could not see me because of bombing. As I mentioned earlier, my parents had prayed for some time after that, fearing I would die in the battle.

"God remembered their prayers!" I concluded.

But the danger of death remained real, as my youngest brother, Aimé learned. Before the conflict began, Aimé had lived near Bacongo, a district of Brazzaville, which was mostly inhabited by residents from the Pool region. But now the Pool region (whose soldiers were called "Ninjas") was at war with most of the rest of Congo's south, including my region. (Non-Pool southerners were called "Niboleks.") These conflicts spilled over into the segregated neighborhoods of Brazzaville.

When the war started, Ninja soldiers began killing many Niboleks in Brazzaville, so Aimé and his Nibolek friends escaped to where Thérèse was living in Diata. One day Aimé decided to visit the youth group in Bacongo; a university student, he also wanted to retrieve some of his abandoned economics books.

Before long, Ninja soldiers stopped him, accusing him of being Nibolek because he did not speak in the special dialect common to their Pool region. "I can't speak your language because I'm from Cameroon," he insisted. Satisfied that he must not be Nibolek, his captors released him, but he never did get his books.

Aimé had not understood the genuinely mortal danger he had been in; after all, he had close friends from the Pool region. Thus he soon planned to return to worship in Bacongo. Thérèse was distraught. "Aimé! Are you mad? It's too dangerous for you to risk this."

"I'll be fine," Aimé insisted. To avoid offending our sister, however, he waited until he thought no one would see him, and then sneaked out with his friend Jean Claude. As he anticipated, they had a wonderful time of worship with their fellow Christians from the Pool region.

As the pair headed back toward Diata, however, Ninja soldiers captured them. Their captors tied their hands behind their backs and blindfolded them, then marched them off into an unbearably putrid house. Thrust into a room, they found themselves stumbling over heavy bags on the floor.

"Why not just liquidate them now?" one soldier suggested. "We can throw them in the river after dark." Had Aimé and Jean Claude wondered about the Ninjas' intention for them, that uncertainty vanished now. Aimé tried to prepare his heart to meet God.

"Let's get more bags first," another soldier retorted. The others shuffled out after him.

Aimé and his friend had already been praying, and when their captors left Aimé called, "Jean Claude! I'm over here. Help me get loose." Following Aimé's voice, his friend stumbled blindly over to him and used his teeth to loosen Aimé's bonds.

Once Aimé was free, he snatched the blindfold from his eyes, ready to release Jean Claude, only to freeze in horror. "Jean

Claude . . . we've been tripping over . . . this room is full of corpses!" The vigilantes had been detaining and killing Niboleks.

Aimé quickly loosened his companion's bonds. Though terrified, he spotted a window, clambered up and jumped out. Just as Jean Claude was climbing through the window after him, the door opened. Before the Ninjas could recognize what was happening and fire, he also leaped down into the tall, dark grass below.

The pair forged their way ahead in the dark through the bush until they found cover behind some houses. The Ninjas were shooting in the air behind them, still searching for them in the tall grass. Out of their sight, however, the two took off running and finally found their way to Diata long after midnight.

It was nearly one a.m. when Aimé returned to Thérèse's home. Much to his surprise, he found his sister still awake. "Of course I'm awake," she chided, exasperated. "I've been praying this whole time for God to bring you home safely."

Even after this local conflict ended, however, regional prejudices made life difficult.

Now that I held a doctorate, it was humiliating to live with my parents in Dolisie, my hometown. Yet I could not find full-time work at our country's only university. "This university is for people from the north," a professor scolded me, even though most students at that time were from the south. Most supervisors in Congo hired only people from their own regions. That ethnocentrism seemed no different from that of a few employers in France who had told me, "We don't hire blacks."

I was frustrated and anxious about the future. Still, I knew that God could surmount such barriers just as He had in France. After a few months I finally found a teaching position in the English Language Program of the U.S. Embassy.

Everyone kept asking me, "What did you do to get that job?"

I would always reply, "I didn't do anything; God did it," and then thank Him quietly for my praying friends.

12

Dangerous Love

In much of traditional Africa, women who do not marry by age 25 are regarded as immoral or cursed or perhaps defective. I was 31 when I returned home, and soon learned that some individuals claimed success in cursing me to singleness.

Others suggested that my standards were too high. A few mocked: "So let your God send you a husband from heaven." Another reasoned: "Why wait for a Christian husband when plenty of others are available?" One even advised: "Just become some married man's concubine. Other single women are doing it. Or be a polygamist's second wife. Given the shortage of available men, you need to be realistic about the alternatives."

The lack of respect for single women in our culture had contributed to my difficulty in finding work, but even when opportunities arose to teach Sunday school or speak publicly about God's Word, those who were involved raised the question of my singleness. Christian friends tried to set me up with various men—some godly and some not.

A New Husband

I still loved Craig, but I realized that he would never express interest in me. I had always dreamed of being loved and having a family; if I wanted to have children, I needed to marry soon. I had been refusing most men's interest, wanting a husband I could trust; I had had such a wonderful father growing up that I actually did have high standards. But soon I grew impatient. Prophecy has to be tested, and I surely could not depend on prophecies that seemed to point to Craig.

Finally Manassé, a man in the church, proposed to me. I had known him in Dolisie when he was not a Christian, but I trusted that he had been genuinely converted afterward as he claimed. There seemed to be few unmarried men available who even claimed to be committed to Christ. Also he was educated, having recently finished his doctoral study in linguistics in Belgium. I was so tired of being ridiculed for my singleness that I finally decided I was being unrealistic and should accept this marriage as God's provision.

And thus I made the most dangerous decision of my life.

We went through all three Congolese weddings (the traditional, legal and church weddings). I paid for almost all of them myself because I was the only one working. Traditionally a price is given to a bride's family to show the groom's financial commitment to her. Contrary to the custom and without my father's knowledge, I gave Manassé the money to pay my bride price.

I did not know that Manassé was a bigamist. Just a few weeks into the marriage, Manassé began staying out late and coming home drunk. He stopped attending church now that he had a Christian bride. He began to speak of following the teachings of a local cult, insisting that one should worship only "the

Great Master of the Universe," not Jesus. He took the money I set aside to give to the church, using it for his drinking, and he began insulting me.

"You didn't merit your doctorate, you retarded whore!" he would shout. I would hide somewhere and cry. I felt helpless, my dreams shattered; far worse, I felt guilty for rushing into the marriage.

By the time I knew that I was pregnant, Manassé was threatening me and physically abusing me. One night he warned, "You haven't seen anything yet! I'll have *really* hurt you when you find yourself in the hospital with a foot or an arm or an eye missing."

Another day he began shouting again, "You're nothing but a stupid prostitute!"

This time I tried to stand up to him. "I am not," I retorted. "I was a virgin when you married me. I have a doctorate just like you. I have a teaching position, and you don't even have work yet."

Enraged by my boldness, he rushed toward me and started strangling me. Unable to breathe, I realized that I might be about to die. Before he could kill me, however, he heard my name being spoken. One of my students passing by the window was mentioning me to her companion. Afraid that she might drop by to visit me and witness his action, he released me.

He had choked me so severely I could not swallow normally for three days. I had now begun to fear for my life. My dreams had crashed into the nightmare lived by many Congolese women.

"So What If Your Baby Dies?"

When I went to check on my pregnancy, Dr. King, a doctor in Brazzaville, advised me that I needed an operation to remove uterine fibroids. "Otherwise your baby will certainly die."

I was planning to follow his instructions until another doctor questioned me. "Why are you having this surgery now? Do you want to abort your baby?"

"Abortion? I'm just going to have the fibroids removed."

The physician summoned a gynecologist who corroborated his warning. "You can't have this operation now without losing your baby."

When Dr. King tried to schedule the surgery, I protested. "I'm not going to do it," I told him, "because it will kill my baby."

Annoyed, Dr. King started ridiculing me. "Oh, so what? So what if the fetus dies? Because you're a Christian you waited till you're this old to have a baby. You think this is a precious baby, but it will die at six months' pregnancy—you'll see."

Most people in Congo were not educated; Dr. King was not accustomed to having anyone reject his counsel.

"I'm a doctor, too," I said, refusing to be intimidated. True, I was not a *medical* doctor, but at least I could stand up for myself. Yet he kept berating me as he rose and quickly showed me to the door. Once I was outside, he slammed it behind me.

I began crying in despair as I stumbled into the midwife section of the hospital. *Is my baby really going to die?* I wondered.

At that moment the head midwife strolled in. "I'll take care of this woman," she announced. She examined me and then, to my surprise, pulled out a Bible and began reading.

"My daughter," the midwife announced, "you'll deliver without any problems. Just find some prayer support for your pregnancy." She and I knew nothing about each other's faith, and I had not told her anything about my dilemma. I left encouraged.

Still, it was not an easy time to be pregnant, even barring Manassé's threats to kill me. Some Christians had seen visions of blood in Brazzaville and Dolisie. I even began dreaming about it myself.

I had taken extra work as an interpreter for a U.S. professional who gave lectures to businesspeople. "War might come to 'Joyland,'" she observed one evening.

A Congolese businessman asked for clarification. "By 'Joyland,' do you mean Congo?" he asked.

The lecturer nodded ominously.

I thought it might take a year before war started. Instead it took only a couple of weeks.

Craig

At long last I was going to experience Africa for myself. My friend Emmanuel Itapson persuaded me to travel to Nigeria to teach, but I had a slightly ulterior additional motive. I was going to connect with a particular African American missionary who, Emmanuel knew, fit what I thought God had showed me about my future wife, especially her heart for the poor, her commitment to sharing Christ and her deep humility. As it turned out, she did not sense that a relationship with me was God's will, so I returned reluctantly to waiting. I held on to the fact that trying to follow God's will does not mean that we will know every step of the future; we simply do our *best* and trust God to work out the details.

Several days after my arrival in Africa, I was finally recovering from jet lag and hoping to get a good night's sleep. I was jarred awake by the sound of assault rifles being fired and tear gas canisters being thrown into the street. Police were chasing university students out of their housing. President Abacha's government controlled the news so tightly that the public had no knowledge of the incident unless they were near the campus that day. After this, some church leaders shared, to my dismay, that they contemplated civil disobedience—though this risked execution. A week later, however, Abacha was dead.

Several believers shared with me accounts of how they had barely escaped martyrdom at the hands of jihadists in recent years. Although Boko Haram now makes global headlines, news of these earlier jihadist attacks rarely reached the outside world.

Meanwhile my mentors in Nigeria, including my friend Emmanuel and American professor Danny McCain, taught me that racial or ethnic conflict is not a uniquely U.S. problem. Different peoples in Nigeria competed and sometimes fought; tribalism is a problem in most of Africa. One book that Danny lent me surveyed many cultures in Africa. It included a chapter on the Congo, and I could think only of Médine as I read it. Because I cared about Médine and had been praying for her to find a good husband, I had been elated to learn of her marriage. My most recent letters to her had been returned due to war in her country, but I resolved to try to contact her again once I returned to the States.

For myself, I had earlier concluded that my future wife would be African American. That made sense of where my life had gone so far. But my new experiences in Africa and my many cross-cultural friendships were leading me to consider that perhaps my wife would be from Africa.

I did not want to think that my openness to that possibility had come tragically too late.

13

Escape from Brazzaville

Médine

Manassé discouraged me from visiting my siblings, Emmanuel, Aimé and Thérèse, who were all living in Brazzaville now. Nevertheless in my despair I finally confided in Emmanuel that Manassé was brutalizing me. Emmanuel was so angry that he intended to find Manassé and beat him, but Thérèse stopped him.

"No, let's pray," she insisted. She suggested that they go pray with Mama Suzanne, who was now in Brazzaville as well. Mama Suzanne's vision cut straight to the point.

"I see Médine in the midst of thorns," she observed. In Congo people sometimes fall into holes filled with long thorns; if no one is available to cut them out they can die there. She turned to Emmanuel. "If you try to pull Médine out the way you want to, she can be hurt or even die."

After they prayed further, she declared, "I can see God's angel cutting the thorns and taking Médine out. Don't try to settle it by human strength. Just pray." Then she added something unusual. "I see Médine getting papers to leave the country. I see a white man, and I hear a voice announcing, 'This is Médine's husband.'"

Emmanuel refrained from informing me of that last part; it made no sense.

Relocating from the Capital

It was safer for me to go out than for my siblings. I was now five months pregnant, and African men consider it disgusting to rape a pregnant woman. Even so, there was little safety. Poorly aimed bullets stray anywhere. One day some soldiers roughed me up even though they knew me from the neighborhood. On top of all of this I was sick with malaria, which triples the rate of miscarriage. I had no access to treatment since Manassé now controlled my money.

Nevertheless I visited my siblings daily. I knew from Emmanuel, whose dwelling was bombed, how dangerous this was. When he and his friend Émile both decided to move to a safer neighborhood, they did not know that our southern soldiers had changed the password. Driving up to a barricade, Emmanuel offered the expired password.

Shaking his head angrily, one of the soldiers barked to his colleague, "Kill these infiltrators. They don't know the password."

Emmanuel froze, but perhaps because the colleague recognized the old password, he hesitated for a few tense moments. Other soldiers were just arriving and one recognized Émile.

"Let these men go," he ordered. "They're southerners." Turning to Emmanuel and Émile, he then observed, "I'm surprised that you weren't gunned down already. The soldiers have been killing a lot of people today."

Manassé was unhappy that I was visiting my family, but he was not at home during the day to stop me. Finally bombing struck even our district; a nearby explosion killed one of the university professors.

"It's too dangerous for a pregnant woman to be there," Emmanuel told me. "We need to get you out."

Emmanuel came and reasoned with Manassé. "Perhaps we should move the women," he suggested diplomatically, "maybe to Dr. Mabiala's apartment." Professor Mabiala was currently away in Canada, but his house and family were on the university campus, which was safer than most locations within the city. Given the current dangers, Manassé had little choice but to agree.

"Médine, are you coming?" Émile, who was driving, called. "We need to hurry."

I paused, my heart pounding. "Manassé, may I really go?" I ventured timidly. He seemed irritated, and I did not want to risk his explosive anger.

"Sure," he consented after a long pause. As quickly as I could I gathered a few clothes and my diplomas. The diplomas represented years of work and could be necessary for finding jobs in the future. I left everything else.

Bombings continued nightly and soon reached even the campus where we were sheltered. One night explosions erupted nearby. "Médine, get under the table!" Emmanuel ordered, helping me; others also dove under furniture. The lights went out as the building shook. Although I was shuddering with fever, I could hear some of my friends crying; others were praying. In the darkness we were all trembling, just as the building was.

After about half an hour the firing stopped, and the lights began functioning again. Most were laughing because we were alive—while crying because we were afraid.

"Médine," Emmanuel said to me, "we have to get you out of here. You're too sick to remain here." Our cousin Leopold, the son of our uncle Prosper, had a contact who could arrange flights. Emmanuel asked him to get me scheduled on a departure out of the capital.

An emergency flight was scheduled to come to Brazzaville. "I can get her name on a list," Leopold assured Emmanuel. Flights were now three times their normal price. War had closed Congo's banks, so Emmanuel could not access his funds there. He pulled together all of his meager resources to try to rescue me.

I was now so sick with chills and headaches and so skinny that Emmanuel feared I might lose the baby. He took me to the only hospital in the capital that was open. After one look at me the nurse grimaced. "This lady is very sick," she said. "She's not going to make it, and the baby's not going to make it, without some strong medicine for malaria." Emmanuel could obtain only some of the medicine for me; it was expensive and limited in supply.

Soon after Emmanuel brought me back to Dr. Mabiala's home to rest, Manassé stumbled onto the campus drunk, accompanied by a distant family member. I was already nauseous; now I was also afraid. Manassé started insulting Emmanuel, who was shielding me from my husband.

"It's *my* wife you seized and brought here," Manassé growled. "I want her to stay with one of my friends from the Pool region."

"I can't do that," I protested, standing up to him. Too often people from different regions had bad relations, and I was too sick to take the risk. "But I can stay with your family," I proposed. This accorded better with African custom.

At this point it was Manassé's companion who intervened. "I don't get it, Manassé. Your wife's sick; she's vomiting; and you want to take her to your friend? He's not even part of your family." He then turned to Emmanuel, affirming, "You're right not to hand her over."

Manassé stared blankly, ashamed. He had not expected his own relative to challenge him.

Airport Under Siege

The next morning Emmanuel made his way to a house owned by Uncle Prosper, where our cousins were staying, to arrange the details of my flight. When he arrived, he saw that Leopold and his siblings were already packed and ready to travel to the airport. "Emmanuel, I'm sorry—we could not get word to you," Leopold apologized. "The plane is scheduled for this afternoon, but we could get Médine only on the second list." That meant that I was registered for the second flight—along with more people than there would be seats for. Besides, there was not room for me in the vehicle.

Emmanuel was panicked. He knew that I was too sick to survive fleeing the capital on foot. "Let me drive your car to go get Médine and then follow you," he urged. "I'll bring your car back to your house afterward." They were skeptical that he could get the car back in time for their own departure, so they did not let him borrow it.

"We can't afford to wait long," they warned. "If you two are coming with us, you'd better hurry."

I was walking distance from them right now, but Emmanuel had to reach me quickly since even walking was difficult for me. He raced back to Dr. Mabiala's apartment at the university. Gasping for breath as he entered, he ordered, "Médine! Eat something and get ready right now." I swallowed hard. I had not expected to have to leave so suddenly without time for goodbyes. Since I was exhausted, I simply threw a few things, including our diplomas, into a small traveling bag.

Emmanuel pressed some cash into my hand. I was so touched by my brother's tenderness that warm tears trickled down my cheeks.

"Emmanuel, you barely have any money left for yourself," I protested weakly. "How will you get out of the city?"

"Médine, you're sick. I'll concern myself with other things later." Then I tried to run back with him, as best as I could, with Emmanuel carrying my bag. It seemed as if the nausea would overwhelm me each step that I took.

Soon after we reached our cousins' home, Matai arrived to escort everyone to the airport. Matai was the ideal contact to ensure safe travel. He worked for Lissouba, the embattled current president, but was also on good terms with partisans of Sassou, the former president now seeking to return to power. The large group waiting there for transportation now crowded into the two cars. Matai would drive the lead car, while Emmanuel would follow driving Leopold's car.

Before getting into the car, Matai turned to my brother solemnly: "Follow me closely. Don't lose me, because if you do you're dead. Only I know the passwords, and the soldiers know only me." Emmanuel nodded apprehensively and stepped into the car.

Passwords indeed proved necessary; Lissouba's southern forces currently controlled most of the road, whereas Sassou's northern forces already controlled the airport. But even passwords could protect us only from deliberate killings, not from stray bullets and random fighting on the airport road. For such obstacles, the best human protection seemed to be speed.

Once we reached the treelined boulevard leading to the airport, we encountered soldiers shooting from both sides. Lissouba's Cocoyes were shooting from one side and Sassou's Cobras were shooting from the other. Matai drove very fast, with Emmanuel racing to keep up. My nausea and dizziness worsened with every wild turn, stop and start that Emmanuel took. I thought I might never get out of that hot, packed car.

Finally we reached the parking area of the airport, but we would still have to make a run for the makeshift emergency terminal out on the airfield. These were tense moments because we heard shooting everywhere. Armed French soldiers protected passengers inside the terminal; no one, however, was standing guard in the parking area.

I was now so faint from fever, pregnancy and lack of adequate food and medication that my head was spinning. I could go no further. I fell far behind the rest of the group.

Emmanuel's eyes grew wide with horror as he looked back to see me lagging behind. "Run, Médine, run!" he called out. I tried, but bullets seemed to be flying everywhere; it felt as though we were running through a hail of bullets. Distress was weakening my resolve even more. Emmanuel ran to me, grabbed my hand and roused my courage to run. We were the last two to reach the shelter. I was on the point of collapse, but we were safe.

No Room on the Flight

Still, our troubles were not over. Once inside the shelter we heard distressing news. Matai turned to us sadly. "There's now only *one* flight to the interior," he said. The second flight, on which I had been scheduled, was cancelled.

In the chaos around us, French soldiers were giving certain information to airport officials. Soon a Congolese official announced loudly, "Those on the second list should go home." That second list had been too long anyway; my name was nowhere near the top.

"Even the single flight is no longer stopping in Dolisie," Matai added. "It's going only to Nkayi."

That meant that that even if I could take the flight, I would still have to take a train or a bus over the rugged roads from Nkayi. No more flights were scheduled after this one for one or two weeks. And if hostilities increased, perhaps none even then.

Emmanuel and I exchanged anguished glances. Already I could barely stand; I would never survive fleeing on foot.

Pathetic though I looked, no one was going to surrender his own seat for me; everyone was preoccupied now with his own survival.

Emmanuel quickly led us in a desperate prayer, pleading for my life. "Please, God, open the door for Médine. She can't endure any more, and the rest of us can't try to escape Brazzaville on foot if she's with us. Please, God, help us! Amen."

14

Fleeing to Dolisie

Médine

While Emmanuel was praying, I could not suppress my fear. We had already been hearing that pregnant women and infants were dying from suffocation on the crowded trains—even without malaria. If I stayed behind, though, I would slow down my siblings in their own escape. Despairing and anxious, I just kept crying out over and over, "Oh, my God, help us! Help us! Please help us!"

Moments later the long-awaited plane from Kinshasa landed. Clearly it was too small for any extra passengers. Taking the first list in his hands, the pilot began calling names rapidly. As their names were called, passengers boarded the plane one at a time. Leopold and his siblings hastily offered their grim farewells, recognizing that I would not be able to fly that day.

I glanced at Emmanuel as if to bid farewell; we both understood that these circumstances likely meant that I would die. I could not survive a more arduous means of escape. Our Lord

Himself warns in the gospels of the hardship refugees face fleeing when pregnant.

Meanwhile, as the pilot continued to call names, Matai appeared restless, scanning the waiting area—as if looking for someone. After what seemed to me like an eternity, the pilot called again one final name, clearly a man's name. No one answered. He called once more.

Matai pivoted toward me abruptly and ordered, "Shout *Here!*"

Without time to understand what was happening, I obeyed. "Here?" I offered timidly, without moving.

"Then come on in," the pilot ordered impatiently, hearing me. "We have to go! What are you waiting for?" Emmanuel handed me the small traveling bag and hugged me goodbye, as we both murmured a brief "Thank You" to the Lord. Finally, after six months of marriage and in great pain emotionally and physically, I was fleeing from the capital for my life.

The final passenger, I boarded the plane, waving to the big brother I was always so close to, not knowing if I would ever see him again. I felt terribly nauseated. I held a small plastic bottle in my hand in case I threw up or needed to spit. As the flight began to taxi down the runway, I prayed, "Lord, please get my brother back safely to the others." I prayed for myself, too; the plane had not yet departed from the war zone.

I learned of my siblings' fate only later. Having delivered the passengers, Emmanuel and Matai raced back through the parking lot to their cars. As they were entering their respective vehicles, ready to leave the airport, Matai repeated his sober warning: "Stick with me. Remember, my friend: If you don't, you're dead. I don't dare stop for anything."

Neither of them could foresee that the car Emmanuel was driving was going to die in the middle of the boulevard's gun battle.

Meanwhile I was being jostled on the small and noisy plane, spitting into my plastic bottle and trying desperately not to vomit. Finally, at 3:45 p.m., after less than an hour in the air, the flight arrived safely at Nkayi's airport, which was unfortunately a fairly long walk from Nkayi itself.

At least there was no shooting here. We all debarked the plane and started walking for the town. Overwhelmed with nausea and fatigue, I felt so ill now that I struggled even to carry my small travel bag and handbag.

The road to town ran through a huge government-owned sugar cane plantation; the sugar cane was so tall I could not see around the bends in the road. I fell far behind and was about to lose sight of the others on the road ahead. Too weak even to call out to them to wait for me, I felt terribly alone and afraid. A human or even animal predator could lurk inside the dense maze of sugar canes. As a lone straggler I was completely defenseless.

Emmanuel was having struggles of his own. He was following Matai closely on the boulevard. With no warning, however, something went wrong with Leopold's car. It slowed to a halt and the engine died. Because there was shooting everywhere, Matai dared not risk his own life by waiting for Emmanuel, so he kept driving.

Panicked, Emmanuel tried desperately to restart the car. No sound came from the engine. He turned the key again, and then again and again, but the car was dead. What could he do? If he got out of the car to run, no direction was safe; trying to run on foot amid the gunfire was suicidal.

Emmanuel resolved to do the only thing he could do: Pray. "Lord, help me! Save me! Lord, please make this car start again." Over and over he turned the key, but nothing happened. He could only continue crying frantically, "Lord, help me! Lord, help me!"

Journey Home

Increasingly feeble, I, too, turned to my only source of help, pleading, "Oh, Lord Jesus, help me!"

At that moment Thierry, a teenage member of the group ahead, noticed that I had fallen behind. He rushed back and took my bag alongside his own heavy one, walking with me. After we had walked some twenty minutes, Leopold, who had hurried ahead, was able to hail a taxi and returned to pick us up.

Once our taxi reached the railroad station, however, we had another rude surprise: The trains were not running. The best we could do was pile into trucks or old vans heading to Dolisie.

Nkayi was already overcrowded with refugees trying to rent space on vehicles going to other towns and villages in the interior. All the refugees were waiting in the marketplace for any chance of transportation. Every time a bus or large truck rolled in, people ran to it and shoved to get a seat or a place to stand. I just sat on the ground, too sick to move, unable to push my way forward and wondering how I could possibly reach Dolisie.

Finally understanding how sick I was, Leopold did his best to help me. "I'd better keep you in the same vehicle that I'll be in," he decided.

Late in the afternoon he was able to find us all places on the same large lumber truck. My cousins crowded into the back of the truck with other travelers, but Leopold persuaded the driver to let me ride in the front. My seat was considerably more expensive than riding in the back of the truck, but since reaching Dolisie now seemed a matter of life and death, I used the money that Emmanuel had given me. Emmanuel's sacrifice reminded me bitterly that my husband, who now controlled all of my possessions, had offered me nothing.

Leopold helped me up into the cab, where I positioned my bag under my feet. Before the truck could pull away, a desperate young mother approached the cab, and the driver welcomed her. Because the cab was elevated, she handed her crying baby, several days old, up to me, then climbed into the front seat beside me. This woman was another refugee from Brazzaville who had made her way to Nkayi. I rocked the baby for a few minutes until the baby was calm.

Only then, when she turned to thank me, did we recognize each other. "Madame!" the young woman cried. She was one of my students from Brazzaville. When she recognized my pathetic condition, she began to weep. Was there no hope for anyone? I encouraged her as best as I could as the truck lurched forward.

We had the best seats on the truck; Leopold and the others in the back lacked any covering. Despite this advantage, my face was soon covered with the dust that characterized the dry season. The truck forged its bumpy way forward slowly; it kept stopping at every village to let people off and sometimes take others on. I could only pray that the truck would reach Dolisie safely as sometimes trucks broke down on the road.

My student got off at a village. "May I get off for a few minutes with her to use the toilet?" I implored the driver.

"I can wait a few minutes," he agreed mercifully, gauging my condition. I climbed down and hobbled off to find the community toilet hole. When some villagers observed how gaunt I appeared despite my swollen belly, they began weeping.

"Is this what we've come to?" one woman lamented. "What lies ahead for our nation?"

Finally, after nightfall, the truck dropped us off in Dolisie. My cousins and I trudged slowly to my parents' house, where my youngest sister, Gracia, was also living with her two children. A stream of refugees had already notified my anxious parents of trouble in Brazzaville. They had temporarily taken in Leopold's sister and her family and awaited the arrival of my cousins.

As I reached the door and my mother's eyes fell on me, she gazed at first, wondering who I was. With a start she recognized me.

She started crying as she ran to me. "My daughter, what has become of you?" Not only was she concerned at how emaciated and fatigued I was, but Emmanuel, Aimé and Thérèse were not with me. "They're still in Brazzaville?" she gasped.

My father at that moment was sitting in the dining room, praying, "Lord, please protect my children." A stroke, brought on by diabetes and high blood pressure, had left him paralyzed on one side of his body so that when he learned of our arrival he could not rise easily to greet us.

"Everyone, come inside," Papa Jacques called out to us. We gathered around him, then he led us in prayer. "Thank You, God, for the safe arrival of one of our children and all of Prosper's children. And God, we pray that You will protect our other children also."

I had not expected to survive the day, but now I was home. I wept as I weakly recounted the day's events. I did not know if Emmanuel had made it safely back from the airport or what would become of my other siblings in the war-torn capital. We were sure that Eliser, at least, was safe in his home in Pointe-Noire.

After I rested for several days, Gracia walked me to the nearby clinic where I received treatment for my malaria.

Family Fugitives

Nine days later we learned the fate of my three siblings left in Brazzaville.

Stranded on the road, Emmanuel kept turning the key in the ignition and praying frantically, "Lord, help me! Lord, help me!" The engine suddenly jerked into life. Emmanuel was sweating. He now had a new problem: Matai was gone. Even if he could remember the roads back, he did not know the passwords.

The most urgent issue was to get out of the embattled boulevard as quickly as possible, but the new danger loomed before him. When he reached the first checkpoint he was amazed that the soldiers waved him through. Apparently Matai had alerted them that he might be coming, just in case Emmanuel survived and restarted the car.

Drenched with sweat, Emmanuel somehow found his way to Uncle Prosper's Brazzaville house. Once he parked the car there, it died again—never to restart.

Emmanuel now trekked back to Dr. Mabiala's apartment, relieved to be alive and to know that I must be on my way to safety. But he, Thérèse and Aimé still had to find the safest means to flee the city. The train was crowded and was not completely safe, but waiting was growing ever more precarious. After three more days of growing instability, they made their way to the edge of the city. Trains could not enter the city now, but were picking up refugees at a stop just outside. An evangelical church nearby was helping those people who were sleeping in the open air at the station.

As they waited, a train arrived. So many refugees sought to force their way on board, however, that my siblings could not get in. That night they and others slept outside, enduring mosquitoes and the alarming noise of gunshots, in hopes of catching the next train. In the morning a bomb hit the station, injuring many.

Shaken but not hurt, my siblings hurried away from the pandemonium to try to find a truck or bus heading for Dolisie. In the market they negotiated with the owners of a fish truck for a ride. The ride was very expensive, exhausting more of Emmanuel's limited savings. But though the trip in the fish truck was difficult, bumpy and stinky, they reached Dolisie the next afternoon.

When Eliser was able to visit from Pointe-Noire, we were overjoyed to be together again.

Fighting in the capital continued for months. Afterward a tense peace settled—for a time. But Dolisie, the country's third largest city, was the home of the ousted president, Lissouba. Dolisie, along with other strategic sites in the south, would soon become the war's next target.

15

Motherhood

Médine

Dreams are valued in Africa. Shortly after I reached Dolisie, Papa Jacques recounted to me a dream from the night before. "I dreamed that an American pastor wanted to marry you, and I happily granted him permission. Then, however, I remembered that you were already married. When I had to inform the pastor, he was sad."

When I heard this, I thought of only one person; but it was now too late. I had not even sought God before marrying Manassé. What had I done?

Dangerous Childbirth

If I had undergone Dr. King's surgery, the baby would have died. And since I would have been in the hospital when war came, I probably would have died, too. Nevertheless I remembered anxiously Dr. King's grim prediction about the child dying. Other doctors in Brazzaville had determined that I would need to have a C-section, something for which I would need to borrow money. In Congo, C-sections were not very safe; during the present instability one might not get antibiotics to heal properly. Many women were dying from infections after C-sections.

The midwife in Dolisie felt that the baby was turned the wrong way for birth. I went to pray with Ma Pauline, Dr. Mabiala's mother-in-law. She felt the Lord speaking: "Manassé isn't going to come back. But the baby will be all right." A few hours afterward, I felt the baby's position turning from sideways to upright.

The doctor soon realized that I would not need a C-section; yet I came close to dying anyway. Medical conditions in Africa are not what they are in the West. On a September day in the harsh conditions of the nation's conflict, I gave birth to a little boy. Because of extreme anxiety, I had not been able to eat for about a day. During my delivery the midwives gave me an episiotomy with no anesthesia; then instead of sewing me up after the birth, they went off to relax, talking and laughing. Only after three hours did they return with a needle and thread, and again, of course, no anesthesia.

After I delivered I passed out twice when they were about to take me from the birthing area into another room. Because I had fainted, the staff left me in the birthing area; I could not understand why I had to remain there so long.

Just as they were finally ready to move me, the doctor came by. Motioning to the room where they planned to take me, he said, "Which of you sanitized this room?" Realizing from their responses that it had not been cleaned yet, he demanded, "Whom did you put in this room?"

"We're about to put this lady in there," the nurse explained, gesturing toward me, "but we haven't gotten to it yet."

"Are you trying to kill this woman?" the doctor shouted. "Somebody just died of yellow fever in that room! You've got to clean the bed before you put anybody in there, especially somebody who's got an open wound from an episiotomy."

My yellow fever immunization was not current, so passing out had possibly saved the baby's life and mine.

Angry Departure

Gradually recovering from my delivery, I eventually managed to pen a short note to Craig, telling him of some of the trials I had been through. I knew that he would continue to pray for my child and me. I also knew that he would be heartbroken over my pain and struggles. The thought of his faithful prayers brought me great comfort.

Like other children, my new little son, whom I named David, often suffered from malaria and attendant convulsions. One day I went with some friends to inquire from a man of God about my son. The man's forehead wrinkled. "Why did you have this child out of wedlock?" he demanded.

"I didn't," I responded, perturbed. "I'm married."

The man seemed perplexed. "I can't see the husband," he noted, confused.

A few weeks after David's birth, we learned that Brazzaville had fallen to the soldiers of Sassou Nguesso, the former president. People from the south, our region, were now fleeing, fearing death. Reports came that soldiers stripped fugitives of anything valuable. It was good that we had escaped when we had.

Two days after Brazzaville's fall, Dolisie itself was in chaos; I was grateful not to be recovering from a C-section. On the one hand, the Mambas (inadequately trained southern soldiers) were shooting all day long, reportedly demanding pay. On the other hand, the Cocoyes (Lissouba's better-trained southern soldiers) were firing back at them. Finally Lissouba fled, and we all hoped that peace would come.

But peace was proving elusive—in more ways than one. Somehow Manassé reached Dolisie, and he confronted my father.

"I came to take my wife," he announced. "I'll send her to stay with my parents in the village."

Although frightened because I had never met his parents and did not know how they would treat me, I was ready to submit to his demand. Papa Jacques, however, having learned how Manassé had abused me, did not want to let him isolate me from all support or protection. In Africa we resolve family disputes by dialogue between the families.

"Manassé, you need to bring your uncle so we can discuss the matter properly," my father said.

Manassé muttered something then stormed away. Soon a military jeep arrived at the house, sending everyone into a panic. One of Manassé's relatives had come to deliver a defiant letter.

"You're naïve," he accused in writing. In Africa only the most tactless person would insult an elder, particularly a father-in-law. Dolisie respected my father, the retired railroad supervisor, as one of its wisest elders. "I don't need to bring anyone with me," the note declared. Manassé was boasting, proud of his European doctorate and political connections.

The next day Manassé returned in person, expecting to take me with him. Papa Jacques refused to be intimidated. "You will talk with Médine only here, outside the house, until you bring your uncle for discussion," he said firmly.

"Look, I don't need your daughter!" Manassé shouted. "Or her baby!"

He did not return.

Angolan Soldiers

A few days after we learned of Brazzaville's fall, the new president's Angolan allies arrived in Dolisie. The day started quietly and in the usual way; everyone had to fetch water for the day, go to the market and cook. We all knew that women were at risk of being raped and the strongest-looking men of being killed, but we could only take our chances. We still had to eat, drink and wash.

Nearly a month had passed since I had given birth and recovered from some complications that attended it, so I was now finally able to walk normally again. Early one afternoon, my little sister, Gracia, and I ventured out to wash dirty clothes, especially David's diapers. In recent months water had rarely come from the faucets; the nearest available water source was the still-working faucets in the not-too-distant downtown area near the high school. Our friends there, the family of Ngoma Boniface, allowed us to use their outside faucet and sink located behind the house. Less than a twenty-minute walk away, the area was near enough that it seemed almost like our own neighborhood.

We switched on the faucet and began washing the clothes by hand, as we always did. Without warning, the sound of gunfire resounded and people in the streets scampered for cover. The shots were so loud and numerous that Gracia and I clasped each other in terror. We could not seek cover inside the house because its owners were not at home and the house was locked. We sheltered behind it for perhaps 45 minutes, praying desperately for God to protect our lives.

As we soon learned, our family heard the shooting and panicked for our safety. "I'm going to get them," Aimé said. He was the strongest family member physically. What a time for his sisters to be washing clothes! He hurried along the dirt path leading past our neighbors' homes and up the rocky dirt road to the high school. From there, the house where we were washing would be within sight across the street.

When he reached the high school, Aimé figured that he could bolt across the street quickly. Preoccupied with the concern of finding us, he sprang forward—only to confront two advancing jeeps full of Angolan soldiers. He stood frozen in place expecting to be gunned down. He knew from experience that in such circumstances soldiers often had orders to kill any man they found.

"God, please forgive my sins," he whispered, "and welcome me to heaven." An earthly voice, however, diverted his attention.

"Come forward," the leader of the soldiers barked in Portuguese, motioning firmly. Aimé stepped forward, hands raised in a sign of surrender. The man began questioning him in broken French, demanding, *"Toi Cocoye?"* ("Are you Cocoye?")

"No," Aimé replied honestly.

"Toi militaro Lissouba?" ("Are you Lissouba's soldier?")

Aimé again replied negatively. The officer examined Aimé's shooting fingers to make sure there was no callous. *"Mais toi . . ."* ("But you . . .") The officer could not find the appropriate French word to describe Aimé's strong shoulders, so he gestured toward them.

"Ah," Aimé replied carefully. He tried to smile and explained with gestures that he exercised a lot and carried heavy loads.

"Amigo!" the officer said with a laugh.

"Amigo!" Aimé responded nervously.

The Angolan commander and his soldiers waved to Aimé as their vehicle started off, leaving him trembling. "God . . . God . . . thank You for sparing my life." He remained transfixed in that spot for a few moments, as gunshots sounded in the distance. He had offered these soldiers no convincing reason not to shoot him. Why had they spared him?

Though dumbfounded, he recalled his mission. He bounded to the back of the Bonifaces' house, finding us huddled with fright. "Grab the clothes and water and follow me," he said, lifting the heaviest pail, full of wet clothes. "I just almost got shot. We have to get out of here!"

As we crossed the main avenue by the high school, we could see fighters in the distance, their faces painted with charcoal. Aimé led us quickly along the dirt path between houses.

Foreign Occupation

About two thousand Angolans and northern Cobras entered Dolisie that fall, and word came to us that they had orders to demolish the city. Apparently, however, because they did not encounter any resistance, they did not execute those orders.

But Dolisie felt like a conquered city. Angolans and Cobras were everywhere in the streets. We had escaped from war in Brazzaville only to find it at our doorstep. Although some northern leaders tried to control the situation, within a few days the conditions deteriorated further. Both Angolans and Cobras executed men, raped women and terrorized the populace. The violent soldiers looked like red-eyed young men under the influence of drugs. Food and everyday staples, while still available, had doubled in price. Stores, hotels and the bank were plundered and burned. Although frightened, I could only entrust our lives to God, writing in my journal, "God has a wonderful plan for all of us."

Despite the occupation, my brothers made their way periodically to the market to buy food. Like other young men, they now wore a piece of white fabric to indicate that they were for peace and not involved in the war. When they returned home, they passed on the news they had heard about raping and killing in other districts. The last Europeans and other foreigners who were living in Dolisie had now fled.

Peace Deteriorates

Our city remained occupied over the next year. I found a small job selling vegetables at the market on Mondays to earn some money to help with David's care. Certain now that Manassé had abandoned David and me, I gave some of the little money I had to a lawyer to file papers for divorce. Even though the situation around us was desperate, there was shame in my life to be a professor and have to sell vegetables.

Gradually Brazzaville became calmer and many displaced workers returned to their jobs there. I could not go back to my job, however, because the embassy where I had worked was now closed. Without a job there I could not afford to relocate to Brazzaville with my baby.

I was soon grateful that I had stayed where I was. Within a couple of months we learned that conflicts had started again in Brazzaville. Soldiers had reportedly begun killing students from the south; many students trekked for weeks to reach Dolisie.

While Brazzaville suffered the worst, the conditions were also becoming intolerable in Dolisie. Word had it that Angolan soldiers and Cobras were now surrounding one district after another, arresting young men and detaining them without cause. Parents then had to pay exorbitant fees to get their sons released. More urgent for me, David was very sick.

Troops were also firing randomly in the city, probably sometimes at each other but often into the air. One late afternoon Papa Jacques was sitting in his armchair when Mama Jacques invited everyone to the table for dinner. He had hobbled on his cane only a few steps from the armchair when a stray bullet pierced the tin roof, passed through his armchair, ricocheted off the floor and went into the wall under the cupboard. Had my father sat in his chair only a few moments longer, he would have been mortally wounded.

Finally, that December, the Cobras and Angolans surrounded our district, arresting many young men. By God's grace, Aimé and Emmanuel were not at home when the soldiers came.

Others proved less fortunate. In the early hours after midnight on the morning of Christmas Day, an Angolan soldier wanted the girlfriend of Raphael, one of my cousins.

"Let her alone," my cousin demanded.

After a brief verbal exchange, the soldier shot him. Raphael cried throughout the night. "Please help me! Someone help me!" His neighbors were afraid to open their doors because of the soldiers. His body was found on the street in the morning.

16

Grasping the Ungraspable

Craig

Mail service out of Dolisie resumed during the brief period of relative peace, and Médine and I were able to correspond for a few months. It was then I learned of her husband's abandonment of her and her son. My heart broke for them.

Médine avoided discussion of war, in case her mail was censored, until the last letter she penned to me. There she wrote that she wanted to tell someone outside what was happening to her and her family. Entrusting that letter to a nephew who was leaving for Côte d'Ivoire, where he was studying, she asked him to mail it to me from there.

When I read her words, I felt utter devastation. Médine's letter anticipated a Rwanda-like genocide, starting with her town's most educated citizens. "Soldiers have been killing people daily. My father and brother barely escaped being shot, and I don't know whether I'm going to live or die," she wrote. I fired off several panicked letters to her, but they were never delivered.

I learned later that by the time her letter reached me, much of Dolisie lay in smoldering ruins.

Terrified that Médine was in danger of death, I prayed more out of anguish than faith. But another tragic realization also gripped me. Was it possible that my caution years before had caused me to make a huge mistake concerning Médine? Was she suffering now for my foolishness and stubbornness? Here was a godly, intelligent, beautiful woman who had felt attracted to me as I had to her. Maybe God had just expected me to use common sense?

Now I wished that I could tell her how much I loved her. I had avoided sharing my feelings—so afraid that she could not endure the deprivation, sacrifice and even contempt often associated with ministry. But that concern seemed absurd now, and I now had more friends who did not pray in tongues than who did.

While I agonized over these things, God's still small voice broke through unexpectedly: *My child, I know how much you care for Médine. I know that you followed what you thought was My will. I will do what is best both for her and for you.*

The promise was no more specific than that, but it comforted my heart. My heavenly Father is trustworthy. Yet as days passed and the living experience of His voice began to fade, my anxiety began to escalate. One friend was confident that Médine could find work in Nigeria if she could get out of Congo, but we had no way to contact her. I solicited prayer support for her from many friends. "It would be better for me to die than her," I pleaded.

Seeing how distraught I was, an African friend tried to help. "If she's still alive, perhaps some of my military friends could send in a security force to rescue her." For a moment the suggestion encouraged me, but then it struck me as both impossible and something that would endanger more lives. We did not even know where she was. Nor, I knew, would she leave without her family.

Afterward I felt God's Spirit chide me: *You were willing to trust in a security force to rescue Médine. How much more should you trust in the Lord of hosts?*

I understood. There was absolutely nothing I could do except trust God—yet God is trustworthy.

Hearing Clearly

Médine remained constantly on my heart and in my prayers. As I was doing the dishes a few days later I heard Him speak again: *I will take care of her, and I will make you a blessing to her. And someday, you and she will minister together in Francophone Africa.*

My heart jumped with hope. Médine had always promised to translate for me if I visited Congo. God's words might be telling me that would happen. And they also, most happily, implied that she would survive the war.

Not every word I received from well-meaning friends was an encouragement though. A young believer prophesied: "Don't have sorrow upon sorrow for Médine, since you both have the hope of eternal life." Though believers have eternity to look forward to, the words discouraged my hope of Médine's survival. I redoubled my prayers after that, clinging desperately to what I thought *I* had heard God say. Not only was I praying desperately for her, but I was also praying that she would experience the comfort of *knowing* that I was praying for her.

While I believe that God speaks to us, our hearing can be partial, subjective and sometimes misleading. During this period several women notified me that God was leading them to marry me; I was sure otherwise. When I prayed about each of these women as a potential spouse, I always heard no. When I prayed about Médine as a spouse I heard only silence. Was the silence because it was not yet the time for me to know the answer? Or was it because the issue could never even arise again?

In any case, my biggest personal prayer request every day was for my friend's safety.

The War in Congo

It helped the agonizing days to try to understand further the situation in Médine's country, but almost nothing was reported in American media. My research helped me understand that Congo-Brazzaville is the smaller, former French Congo, which supported free France in its campaign against the Nazis. Demographically it is much like its larger neighbor and namesake on the other side of the Congo River. Part of the country is overgrown tropical rainforest, what some Westerners might call jungle. Locally people call it simply "the forest." Dirt roads connect many villages there.

Denis Sassou Nguesso, a military officer from the north, was president of Congo until the early 1990s when democratic elections brought to power Pascal Lissouba, a professor from the more populated south of the country. Lissouba wanted to renegotiate Congo's oil contracts given to the French company Elf Petroleum, complaining that France reaped more profit than Congo did. Elf Petroleum, fiercely competitive in the international market, was later implicated in backing Lissouba's overthrow. Angola, which worked closely with Elf, supported Sassou, a coalition that effectively sealed Lissouba's fate. France's president maintained his long-standing friendship with Sassou; many Africans believed he supported Sassou's new bid for power.

Partisans of each leader blamed the other for provoking war. In any case, both sides were heavily armed before it started, during a period of instability throughout Central Africa. Before its end, this war would cost tens of thousands of lives and make refugees of hundreds of thousands of others. (In contrast to more technical language, people in Congo referred broadly to

121

refugees as displaced fugitives needing refuge, both those who crossed into Gabon and those who did not.)

As the months passed I hoped that the reports I was able to dig up were exaggerated; after all, how could such dramatic events be occurring without U.S. media reporting them? The newsmagazine to which I then subscribed did not even report the war in the neighboring country of Congo-Kinshasa until an estimated two million people had died there. Had one percent of those casualties been in Europe or North America, it would have been front-page news. Apparently the sexual antics of Hollywood figures generated higher ratings than the lives of thousands of Africans. In time I ran across reports from the International Red Cross and other charitable organizations.

During most genocides, the world refuses to acknowledge and believe it until it is too late. "Deliver those who are being led away to slaughter!" the Bible warns. "If you say, 'We didn't know what was happening!' doesn't the true Judge see your heart? Won't he pay you what you deserve?" (Proverbs 24:11–12).

After each round of genocide, the world declares, "Never again!" We said it after the Turkish genocide against Armenians, after Hitler's genocide against the Jewish people (and the Roma people and others), and after Pol Pot's genocide in Cambodia. After the Rwandan genocide, the West again proclaimed, "This must never happen again!"—ignoring the fact that now in the late 1990s the atrocities had simply moved into the larger Congo.

I did not know Médine's fate during those long months. She and her family were in the midst of a brutal war, and all I could do was wait.

17

Confronting Soldiers

Médine

About two weeks after my cousin was shot to death in the street, Dr. Mabiala's wife, Henriette, traveled to Dolisie to visit her mother, Pauline, and reported to us an unsettling prophecy that she had been given. "I wanted to move here to Dolisie," Henriette said, "but the prophet was adamant. 'Don't stay more than two weeks. If you stay past midnight, Sunday, January 24, you won't be able to get out.'"

Henriette grimaced. "You all need to leave."

We were panicked. But where could we go with our disabled father? Certainly I did not want to have to flee war again. Perhaps through prayer the trouble could be delayed. We decided to stay as long as we could.

Less than a week after Henriette spoke to us, refugees with swollen feet began crowding into Dolisie. They had walked for more than a month after escaping fighting in Brazzaville, often surviving by picking mangoes or because of charity from

123

some people in the Pool region. Some of my family members took the risk to travel. Emmanuel left town to visit a friend in Les Saras, planning to return on January 25. Eliser left for his residence in Pointe-Noire. Their departures left Aimé the only able-bodied man in the household.

On Sunday, January 24, I was praying with Fanny, Henriette's niece.

"War is very near," Fanny said, speaking prophetically. "When it first touches you, though, you mustn't flee in the panic of the moment. You need to trust God to protect you. But I see soldiers in front of your house." She paused, and then spoke with assurance: "Difficult times are coming, but many people, including many white people, are praying for you."

This final portion must have seemed strange to Fanny since Congo was almost completely black, especially now. "Do you have many white friends?" she asked curiously.

I nodded.

Monday morning, the day about which the prophecy warned, began calmly. Thérèse was preparing to leave for the elementary school where she taught. Gracia was getting ready for school, as were her ten-year-old daughter, Praise, and nine-year-old son, Lud. Nelly, our teenage cousin who had been living with us, was also preparing to leave for school. Poor Nelly had left her town, Mossendjo, to come and study in Dolisie. Now she was trapped with us in this war.

At six in the morning, however, we heard a deafening noise. It sounded as if Dolisie was being bombarded. Happily for us, no one had left our house yet.

At seven o'clock armed men with their faces either painted black or veiled with masks of black cloth began entering the district. These were our southern soldiers; they were ordering residents to vacate the area.

"We will be fighting in the streets," they warned.

Confusion and panic ensued with people scurrying in all directions, carrying bags and sleeping mats on their heads. Small children were crying, and parents were running after older children who had started for school. Yet we could not flee with Papa Jacques paralyzed; we could only trust the Lord's reassurance from His word of prophecy the day before. After bidding goodbye to our departing neighbors, we went back inside and prayed anxiously for protection.

By eight o'clock our district appeared empty, as if we were the only people there. The only noise audible now was shooting and bombing.

By ten o'clock we could feel the reverberation of explosions, likely from missiles. It grew so intense that the house began to shake; I feared our doors and windows would shatter. The only member of the household who was not afraid was David, who, now sixteen months old, was thankfully healthy at the moment. Every time he heard an explosion, he would shout joyfully!

My family did not share his enthusiasm. "The soldiers will hear him," Aimé warned.

"Can't you breastfeed him to keep him quiet?" Thérèse pleaded.

Though I had been weaning him, I complied with her request for the sake of our safety.

Our biggest concern was Papa Jacques. Although he seemed calm, we were anxious about his dangerously high blood pressure. And where was Emmanuel, who had not returned yet as he had planned? His absence added to our worries. Hours passed slowly that day, and explosions and gunfire shaking the home made it hard to sleep that night. Despite our anxiety, however, we somehow felt a deep assurance that God was watching over us.

Rising Tensions

After the disruptive night, an eerie quiet settled over our district. We prayed and debated again what to do. Carrying Papa

Jacques into the rainforest seemed suicidal. And how could I hide there with a toddler? David did not know how to stop talking, shouting or crying.

We mostly stayed inside. At one point my friend Yvette burst in, distraught. "My brother fled with my baby!" she cried. "I don't know which direction they went." In her panic, she had left her home without shoes. "Take these flip-flops," I urged, and prayed with her for the safety of her eight-month-old child. As Yvette departed I contemplated anxiously my own baby's safety.

Several hours later, Ngoma Boniface arrived at our door with thirteen members of his extended family, including sixteen-year-old Massala, who spoke only Lingala, the language of the north. Massala would have to be particularly careful, since southern troops arrested as infiltrators anyone who could not speak the local language.

"There's too much gunfire in our part of the city right now," Mr. Boniface explained. "Might we stay here for the moment?"

"Of course," my hospitable father assured them. This addition brought the total number of people crowded into our little house to 24.

Before long another fugitive reported what was happening in nearby districts. Northern soldiers and Angolans were going from house to house raping women and killing men. The numbers of soldiers from both sides were now swelling.

"We won't go outside more than needed," Papa Jacques determined, hoping to keep our presence quiet. This was going to be a considerable problem because we no longer had running water and would need to use the outside toilet. It took very little time for this situation to prove how dangerous our position was.

It was growing dark when Massala needed to use the toilet. "Aimé," Papa Jacques called. "Go with our guest and stand watch."

126

Just as Massala emerged from the outdoor toilet, two soldiers passing by on the dirt road spotted them. "Stop! Put your hands up," they ordered.

There was no time to think. Massala, speaking in Lingala, yelled to Aimé to run. They dashed madly into the house.

"Soldiers saw us!" Aimé shouted, throwing us all into a panic as he scrambled for cover.

Robbed by Soldiers

Within seconds a loud banging sounded from our wooden back door. As Papa Jacques shuffled to the door leaning on his cane, my mother opened it. Together they stepped out, hoping that the soldiers might show traditional African respect for the elderly. Because I hoped that they might also show compassion on nursing mothers, I followed, clutching David in my arms. Meanwhile Thérèse was crowding everyone else into Gracia's room—the room furthest from the back door.

I sighed with relief as I realized that the armed men were Cocoyes, soldiers from the south. But even though their expressions were at first difficult to make out behind their black painted faces, these soldiers proved antagonistic.

"You're hiding Cobras," one charged. "We heard one shouting in Lingala."

"There are no Cobras here," Papa Jacques explained. His voice managed to remain calm.

"All right, then show us the two boys who ran into your house a minute ago," the soldier retorted.

I was frightened for everyone. "One moment," I requested. Taking a deep breath, I stepped uncertainly back inside the dark home. "Aimé," I called with firmness, "bring your friend out." I hoped that if we cooperated they would not force their way in.

When Aimé and Massala emerged unarmed, the soldiers seemed satisfied that they were not Cobras. "You were lucky," one of the soldiers scolded them. "We almost shot you for running away."

But the other soldier was not finished with us. "Surely you're hiding some Cobras somewhere," he said. "Why else have you refused our militia's orders for civilians to leave?"

My temper began rising. These were soldiers from the south; they were supposed to protect us. I responded with indignation. "We're not hiding anything. My father is barely able to walk. You can see that. He would never make it in the forest. That is why we can't just run off. We can't leave him alone and defenseless when the fighting starts."

I had the fighter's attention, but not the kind of attention I wanted. "I know why *you're* here," he said with a sneer. "You're the girlfriend of one of the northern soldiers." In Congo holding a baby with no husband in sight left me vulnerable to such charges.

"That's not true," I snapped angrily. I had been through too much to have my integrity insulted and, without stopping to think, I ignored the consequences of standing up to armed men.

Unaccustomed to being defied, the soldier, now enraged, lunged to strike me.

Perhaps because of the baby in my arms, however, his colleague abruptly intervened. "Let's let her alone for now," he said. "Why don't we inspect this home?"

The angry soldier lowered his arm and both entered the house. They immediately found something to interest them.

"This old man is rich," the second fighter announced delightedly. "Look at this food. And look here. A television . . . telephone . . . even a stove."

Emerging from our home, he spun quickly toward Papa Jacques. "We need 300,000 CFA—now." That was about six hundred U.S dollars.

My father was taken aback. "We don't have that kind of money," he responded. He had been saving money to buy more food but it was not anywhere close to that amount.

"We can give you six dollars," Mama Jacques offered hopefully. The soldier who had threatened me cursed with fury and fired his gun apparently randomly. Glass shattered, and Papa Jacques crumpled to the ground. Mama Jacques began sobbing as she rushed to him.

Exasperated, I confronted the soldiers again. "How can you be so heartless? You're supposed to protect us." But as I heard my father groan, my anger melted into fear that my father was wounded, and I started weeping. Little David joined in the crying as Mama Jacques tried to help Papa Jacques to his feet.

"I'm all right," he was saying. Papa Jacques had lost his balance, but the bullet had not hit him.

Meanwhile the enraged soldier was still demanding, "You'd better give us six hundred dollars. Now!" He had worked himself into such a rage that I was sure we would all be killed.

So this is how it's going to end, I lamented. *Our own soldiers shooting us.*

"We honestly don't have that much money," Mama Jacques said, her voice sounding desperate.

The calmer soldier abruptly broke the impasse.

"Give us sixty dollars and we'll leave you alone," he said.

"We won't have enough left for food," Mama Jacques protested weakly.

Papa Jacques gestured to her to get the food money. "The next bullet won't miss, Antoinette," he murmured quietly.

She hesitated, then nodded and disappeared into the house. Emerging moments later, she handed the money to the Cocoyes.

They smiled, satisfied, and departed into the night.

18

Planning Escape

Médine

Time was running out. All 24 of us were huddled together in the dining room, shaken but unhurt. "The soldiers know we're here," I said quietly, "and the next time they might want more than money."

"We have to do something soon," Thérèse agreed. "But for now, the best we can do is try to get some sleep." It was already approaching midnight, and the neighborhood, dark without power and nearly abandoned, lay still. Yet my stomach felt more and more unsteady with every gunshot or explosion. Gracia and I spent much of the night using the indoor toilet, despite the lack of running water.

Early the next morning, just after sunrise, everyone gathered again in the dining room to pray and decide what to do.

"Because the soldiers got money," Mama Jacques pointed out, "they'll be back for more."

"And soon the northern fighters will arrive," Mr. Boniface warned. "I'm afraid my family had better head north toward

Mossendjo." Mossendjo was the town where he and Papa Jacques were from. "We'll just take our chances seeking refuge in the villages along the way."

Papa Jacques nodded solemnly and then, glancing toward his son, observed, "This war's chief targets are young men." He paused, but there was no alternative. "Aimé, you need to go with them."

Aimé swallowed hard as his father's words sank in. It would not be easy to leave his family behind, but we all knew that Papa Jacques was right. Papa Jacques led the family in prayer, and then Mr. Boniface and his large group departed.

What to Take? What to Leave?

I felt all the more desperate looking at the eight faces around me. All able-bodied men were now gone. The only way we could flee with Papa Jacques was to carry him, and we did not have anyone left who was strong enough to do that. At the same time, food and water were running low. We could not hold out much longer.

Thérèse broke the silence. "We'd better start deciding what we need to take with us in case we have to leave in a hurry," she advised.

As we began packing, Mama Jacques placed Papa Jacques's medicines on the dining room table so we would not forget them when we left. Trying to travel would be hard enough on him; without his medicines he surely would not survive.

Meanwhile I hardly knew what to take. I added to my travel bag my new Bible and also my journal so I could keep taking notes about the war. Somehow taking notes gave me a way to process what was happening. I gazed at my guitar, camera, books, clothes and all the belongings I had brought from France—as if saying goodbye to them. We packed all our identification documents in a small handbag, although Emmanuel's were missing. We would need these documents if we ever needed to leave the country.

As everyone quietly went about deciding what to take and what to leave behind, a new barrage of rifle fire and explosions not far from the house beckoned us to hurry. Yet the unspoken question remained: When it came time to leave, what would we do with Papa Jacques?

The Prayer

Sensing the growing tenseness in his house, Papa Jacques called his wife to his room. "Antoinette, let's pray." Papa Jacques always prayed concisely yet with great faith. "If You want us to leave this place," Papa Jacques pleaded, "send someone to help us escape—whether on the side of the north or the south. Amen."

No sooner had he concluded his prayer than short taps came at the door. It was the sound everyone had dreaded. Everyone—except Mama Jacques.

"Open it," she instructed, hurrying into the living room as the knocking grew more insistent. "Don't be afraid. We just asked God to send someone to help."

Knowing my mother's faith, I mustered courage to open the door.

But as the door opened, even Mama Jacques was dumbfounded. It was Zonzon, Papa Jacques's nephew. No one could have surprised us more. He and Papa Jacques had fallen out a few months earlier over Papa Jacques's inheritance arrangements.

This will sound odd to Westerners, but under traditional custom in the villages, the eldest nephew inherits his uncle's property even if the uncle has children. It is a practice that often leaves widows destitute. Papa Jacques, however, insisted that he would not follow that practice but would follow national law, which grants the property to the immediate family. This angered Zonzon, who vowed never to visit us again. Of all people to be an answer to Papa Jacques's prayer! But here he was, returning to his uncle's house and offering to help.

"We must go now. It's too dangerous to stay," Zonzon said. "The Cobras are coming and will kill everyone left here."

Our bags were now ready, but we could not leave quite yet. Papa Jacques summoned us to the dining room. "Let's pray," he said. As always my father prayed concisely, entrusting our lives to God's kindness. "Thank You, God, for sending Zonzon. Please give us continued safety."

As we concluded with "Amen," Zonzon surveyed the situation. "I won't be able to carry Papa Jacques," he said, shocking us. But before anyone could reply, Zonzon turned to me. "The wheelbarrow," he ordered. "Get it."

Zonzon helped Papa Jacques into our wheelbarrow. It was now about 9:30 a.m. Though most of the city's other residents were fleeing along the rail lines, we would have to take the road because we could not use the wheelbarrow on stones or rails. We were the last stragglers to abandon our neighborhood, even as many buildings in Dolisie were erupting into flames behind us. We hoped to find at least temporary shelter in villages ahead.

Gunfire and explosions continued to ring out as we hastened up the hill along the dirt road by our home. Besides David, my parents, Thérèse, Gracia, Nelly and Zonzon, our group included Gracia's young children, Praise and Lud. David was strapped to my back; each of us adults struggled with baggage on our heads. I could not see well because my glasses had recently broken and I had only my weaker old ones.

As we plodded forward, we could hear gunfire and explosions off in the distance. Everything else was quiet as we made our way past empty homes. When we reached the middle school and began crossing an open field, Mama Jacques shrieked.

In our excitement about the wheelbarrow, the medicines had been left behind.

19

Life As Refugees Begins

What were we to do? As we deliberated, Papa Jacques interrupted.

"Nobody is going back," he said. "Nobody is going to die for me. If I've got to die, I'll go to my Father in heaven. If not, God will watch over me."

Reluctantly we acquiesced. We had already spent too much time standing in an open space where we made easy targets for marksmen; we needed to move on. Surely war would end soon and we could return to our home?

Finding Aimé!

Shortly beyond the middle school we reached the Bridge Market where I had worked selling vegetables. Many bullet casings littered the ground here; we guessed that this was the scene of the gun battle we had heard a few minutes before. Fearing that soldiers could be nearby, we hurried on.

Eventually we began to make our way up Mount Hammar, from which we could see much of suffering Dolisie in the valley below. The tropical sun beat down directly on us now; its heat and the climb made our loads feel heavier. We were sweating, thirsty and breathing hard. Mama Jacques walked slowly beside the wheelbarrow where her husband lay sweating. He used his functional arm to hold on to the wheelbarrow and stay balanced.

As we reached the top of the mountain, we could see people streaming from every direction with bags on their heads or backs. Suddenly Praise cried out. "Hey, that looks like Uncle Aimé." She pointed toward someone standing with his back toward us.

"The sun is making you hallucinate, Praise," Gracia chided. "By now Aimé is in a distant village with Mr. Boniface's family."

Praise and Lud ran on ahead, however, and began shouting excitedly, "Uncle Aimé! Uncle Aimé!" It was true; God had reunited us. We laughed and cried, as he joined us. He took over pushing the wheelbarrow from Zonzon, who was visibly exhausted.

As we rested under a palm tree a few minutes later, we bombarded Aimé with questions. He explained that he had decided to come back and help us, but once he reached the market his heart started pounding as if something bad was about to happen. As he turned and hurried back up the mountain, heavy gunfire resounded behind him.

We rested there, contemplating how God had helped not only Aimé but the rest of us as well. Had we left just a few minutes earlier, we would have been caught in the crossfire. Had Zonzon come just a few minutes later, he never would have reached us alive.

We temporarily adopted some others into our group who had gotten separated from their families during the chaos. As we resumed our trek, the road became too uneven at some points to push the wheelbarrow with Papa Jacques in it. Muscular

Aimé hoisted Papa Jacques onto his back. There were reasons that we affectionately called him our "international strength."

Risks for Vegetables

Late that afternoon, after passing other small villages, we finally reached Ngoyo. Zonzon joined his family to stay with the village chief, while Aimé's friend Modé invited him to spend the night with him in one of the houses in front of the church.

The rest of us parked our mats and other belongings on the floor of Ngoyo's Catholic church, along with many other refugees. The church's windows, like those of most other buildings, lacked screens or glass to keep mosquitoes out. As nightfall approached, we arranged our mats on the floor beneath the church benches, draping our mosquito nets over the benches—our only protection against the risk of malaria. Some mosquitoes got in and bit us anyway, but we were too tired to notice.

The next morning I was talking with Ya Bertheline, Modé's mother. She was a nurse who lived in Hammar and regularly helped Papa Jacques. She had fled here to Ngoyo with her two sons along with nearly all her patients.

"I'm heading to my vegetable field," Bertheline offered. "It's in the forest behind Hammar. Would you like to join me?"

"I'm so grateful," I answered; we were out of food. I entrusted David to my sisters and followed.

After we had loaded our large baskets with corn, green leafy vegetables and cassava roots (yucca), Bertheline issued a further invitation. "Médine, come with me to my house in Hammar. I've got some more food there and cooking pans."

That sounded a little too close to Dolisie for safety. "Ya Bertheline, I don't think that's a good idea," I responded.

"It'll be fine," Bertheline insisted. "You don't hear any shooting, do you?" Unable to dissuade her, I accompanied her. As we proceeded, however, we kept running into fugitives from

Dolisie and Hammar. "Don't go back there," they warned. I was also unnerved as we passed the body of a man who had died from gunshot wounds.

"They're being overly cautious," Bertheline insisted. "Look, we can still see people walking around." My discomfort, however, was mounting. A few minutes further down the road we stopped by the house of an elderly woman, one of Bertheline's patients. She was too old and sick to leave. When she recognized Bertheline's voice at the door, she welcomed us in but quickly warned Bertheline with a trembling voice, "Don't go back to your house. I've been having dreams about danger in your house, especially to your older son, Modé. Warn him not to return to your house, no matter what." The warning made sense; soldiers viewed young men as the greatest threat, so they were at the greatest risk of being killed.

"Let's go back to Ngoyo," I urged as we left this house.

"Médine, we'll just go to my house for a couple minutes to gather some things. . . ."

"Ya Bertheline, I'm not going any further," I insisted firmly. "We need to go back." After much discussion my resolve finally won out, so we both returned for our baskets, which we had left in the field.

Dangers to Civilians

Rumors proliferated.

"They're saying Dolisie is safe now," one reported.

"No," another maintained. "The Angolans are still there. If our soldiers lose, we would all need to flee again."

I shuddered hearing that comment; how could we all flee again? But even the most basic needs were getting increasingly difficult to accommodate.

We had been using a slightly secluded hole in the ground as a toilet, but that afternoon the property's owner chased us away. The only alternative was to enter the rainforest and be exposed to snakes and insects. "Please, at least let my father use the place," I begged desperately. "He has his own toilet. He just needs some privacy for the sake of his dignity."

"It's my property," the owner retorted. "I don't want any more refugees using it." I felt exasperated and helpless to protect my father. But none of Ngoyo was secure, as a low-flying military aircraft reminded us a few hours later when it sent everyone scurrying for cover.

The next morning the evangelist Ndimina, who was close friends with Papa Jacques, gathered us for prayer. Papa Jacques spotted Aimé, who had been gone for a few hours. "Come join us for prayer," he called.

"Where have you been, Aimé?" Mama Jacques asked.

"Modé asked me to go with him to Hammar," Aimé explained, "to get some things from their home. But after a couple miles I felt really uneasy about going further." Aimé could not persuade Modé to return to Ngoyo with him. We were all worried for his friend's safety.

Uprooted Again

Early that afternoon undisciplined southern Mambas passed through Ngoyo with their plunder, firing off their guns everywhere. They shot at the refugees' bags and into the air simply to terrorize us. In the midst of the confusion someone brought a frightening report: "The Cocoye have abandoned the war! Angolans are advancing past Hammar." The talk now was that soldiers were executing males between the ages of five and 45.

Only about a decade younger than my father, Zonzon was too "old" to be targeted. But Lud was nine, and Aimé in particular would be in danger.

We all exchanged grim glances. After several moments of uncomfortable silence, Aimé announced, "I'm afraid I'd better move on." He had already had even more close calls than I have had space to mention.

"Go, my son," Papa Jacques urged him. "God be with you. We will keep Lud with us." Then he added, "We had better start moving also." Our small camp of refugees was already in panic from the report.

"I can't travel with you," Bertheline said with fear in her voice, as we told her our plans. "I just learned that Modé went back to Hammar. If I don't hear from him before tomorrow, I'm going back to our home." Modé, not yet thirty, was the man of the household, on whom she depended. Her other, teenage son remained with the other refugees.

As we gathered our meager belongings, I overheard a soldier nicknamed Sous-off, once our uncle's bodyguard, telling Zonzon, "I must go back to Dolisie." Only later would I realize the significance of this comment.

Because Aimé was no longer with us, Zonzon began pushing Papa Jacques's wheelbarrow again. Nearly all the refugees were now streaming toward the next village carrying their heavy loads. I could not hold back my tears as I watched people leaving behind everything they had worked for, sometimes being separated from their loved ones. Meanwhile we climbed steep hills with no shade.

Finally we arrived at the next village, Mafoubou, and settled on the dirt floor of an elementary school. Mosquitoes made sleep difficult this night, but at least no gunfire troubled us. In the morning, however, we could hear the renewed conflict in now-distant Dolisie. I prayed anxiously for Emmanuel and Eliser; they would have no idea where we were.

Heavy rain fell all morning, detaining in Mafoubou the fugitives who wanted to continue farther. Around mid-morning we heard a woman wailing loudly. Thérèse and I went outside the school and found Bertheline falling in the mud as she wept.

"I found Modé," she sobbed. "Angolans . . . shot him dead . . . in front of our house." She had found him face down, shot in the back, his arms full of the food he had gone back to retrieve. Northern soldiers had surrounded Bertheline there, but some members of her tribe who were now working with the north told her to go on; they would bury her son. "They didn't burn my house," she said through her tears, "but I'll never feel able to live there again."

We all embraced her and brought her inside, crying with her for a long time.

That evening a little group of us who had begun gathering for prayer with the evangelist Ndimina gathered around Bertheline. We also collected some money from our meager reserves to help her. As we prayed, Ndimina said that God was telling us to leave this village as quickly as possible because we were not safe here. Since he would be heading toward his own village the next day, he asked Mama Jacques to lead the group in prayer from now on. Then he taught us a song to encourage us: "Everything has its time. Don't think that Father God doesn't have eyes or ears, or lacks understanding. No, everything has its time."

20

On the Run Again

Médine

The rumor that Angolans were advancing past Hammar proved to be false, but Aimé had left and there was no way to reach him. Meanwhile we had no idea where Emmanuel might be; fighting started in Dolisie the day that he was supposed to arrive there, and if he was alive contact was impossible.

Very early Sunday morning on the last day of January, we said goodbye to the evangelist and began walking toward the village of Tao-tao. Zonzon was pushing Papa Jacques in the wheelbarrow quite slowly now; the uneven dirt road with its holes and ruts remained muddy and slippery. After ascending one mountain, we were exhausted and stopped at a crossroads to rest. A pregnant woman, advancing with great difficulty, caught my eye. "I understand," I whispered, shutting my eyes to pray for her.

Once we reached the outskirts of Tao-tao, Mama Jacques led us in thanksgiving. Then Zonzon joined others moving into schoolrooms, and twenty of us settled in part of the small village infirmary. The family of Papa Jacques's friend Dr. Nkaya, a pediatrician, plus Mr. Ibouanga, the assistant doctor, were staying in the only two other rooms in this infirmary.

While my parents went ahead to the local church for the morning service, I made my way to the market to buy some food. In contrast to other villages, Tao-tao had inflated its food prices to get as much from the refugees as possible. I nicknamed Tao-tao "the Wicked Village." How long could our money hold out?

My regular role was feeding our group. That night I again fed nineteen people with the limited food available. I served the children first, then the sick people, then the others and last of all myself. Throughout each afternoon we could only wait hungrily for the time to pass so we could eat. Ever since leaving Dolisie, we had to wait till four or five in the afternoon for our one daily meal, and its nourishment, often meager, would have to last until the same time the next day. Food often filled our dreams at night.

As night settled in, we positioned our mats on the dirty infirmary floor; Mama Jacques exhorted us and led us in prayer before we retired. As many as possible slept on each mat; some could not fit at all. No benches were available, so we draped the mosquito nets over our bags to cover us. As usual our sleep was troubled by gunfire, mosquito bites, stiffness and aching.

Mama Jacques led everyone in the infirmary in devotions every morning and evening. Once as many as 75 people crowded in for prayer; as refugees, we had nowhere else to turn but God.

Since the infirmary had no facilities for handling human waste, we had to go to the toilet in the rainforest. We soon discovered that we did not have to spend much time cleaning up there, though; almost as soon as we had finished, local pigs rushed in to gobble up our excrement. I decided that I would never eat pork again!

Dr. Nkaya was helping wounded women and children as best he could with no anesthesia, but he had a special bond with my father. One day he found Papa Jacques's blood pressure dangerously high. "Jacques, my friend, I brought medicine for my own blood pressure," he said. "But for Jacques Moussounga, I'll share it."

We wondered if something had happened to cause his blood pressure to rise so dangerously. We soon learned the story.

While the rest of us were away, Zonzon had gone to Papa Jacques and begun insulting him. "I should inherit your house!" Zonzon yelled. "That's what tradition demands!"

When he finished his tirade, Papa Jacques replied calmly, "Thank you." Zonzon left in anger.

We were very upset by this. How could Zonzon treat our father that way? And how could we trust him?

A couple of days later, I walked on to Moubotsi, the next village, with some friends. The distance was thirteen or fourteen miles, but food was cheaper there than in Tao-tao. Later, after I returned fatigued, Zonzon placed his hand on David's head.

"You think you're smart," Zonzon said, "but you're stupid."

I brushed off Zonzon's hand, remembering the biblical proverb, "A curse undeserved has no effect." Zonzon appeared to be looking for trouble, but we would simply continue to pray. War was no time to deal with family disputes. Nevertheless David cried a lot that night.

Hidden Motives

Many refugees were now moving past Tao-tao to more distant villages, but because it was difficult to move Papa Jacques, we stayed in this "Wicked Village" for two weeks.

"I need to go on ahead," Zonzon announced one morning. "In Mont-Bello we can hope to find a vehicle traveling home to Mossendjo." Mont-Bello was two villages beyond Tao-tao;

Mossendjo was the extended family's hometown where Papa Jacques was originally from. "I'm coming back to get Papa Jacques," he promised.

We became anxious about this declaration. Thérèse voiced our thoughts. "We can't let Zonzon separate us from Papa Jacques," she said. "He needs us to care for him. He's in no condition to be hurried over these rough paths."

An even more terrible thought had occurred to me. "Given Zonzon's behavior," I said, "he might even want to hasten our father's death."

Thérèse sat quietly for a moment. "Especially in an area like Mossendjo where traditional custom would be followed," she agreed. "That way Zonzon could inherit Papa Jacques's property after all."

"But what is the alternative?" Mama Jacques concluded with a sad shrug. "None of us has the strength to push the wheelbarrow."

That evening during prayer, Pastor Nziengue's wife, Mama Cathy, sensed the Lord speaking. "Papa Jacques should not go to Mossendjo," she told us. "Danger awaits him there."

Papa Jacques nodded. "Well, then, it's settled. When Zonzon returns for me, I'll refuse to go with him."

But how could we move on from Tao-tao by ourselves? We prayed.

The next day David, like some of the other refugees, had diarrhea and high fever. In Africa diarrhea sometimes kills children by dehydration; drinking dirty water can actually worsen dehydration by fostering more diarrhea. When we went to fetch water that morning, a compassionate young deaf man tried to signal something to us about the water we had been directed to. A not-so-kind woman, however, intervened. "You're not coming here again!" she said. "The drinking water is for villagers and their friends only."

"The Wicked Village," I murmured, discouraged. Yet war would ravage proud villages as well as hospitable ones, and some people in the church here were kind. As we were returning to the infirmary without water, I kept pondering the deaf young man's signals; something was clearly wrong. I asked a better-informed refugee.

"These people have been giving you the wrong information," she explained. "You've been drinking from the dirty water well used for cleaning." No wonder we felt sick! She pointed us to a nearer stream of drinkable water, though refugees were using it for both bathing and drinking.

Good News, Bad News

It was late morning when we finally returned to the clinic to find an elated crowd gathered together. I could hardly believe what I was seeing. There stood Emmanuel in the midst of them.

"God has answered our prayers for Papa Jacques," I announced with joy. The very day after Zonzon was no longer with us to push the wheelbarrow, Emmanuel had arrived.

Mama Jacques had been in the infirmary cooking our one meal for the day when he had entered. Turning and seeing him, she had exclaimed, "Emmanuel! Why have you joined us in the lions' den?"

He had simply embraced her with a big smile. After learning of the fighting in Dolisie, he had joined up with two others who had also decided to go look for their families. After difficult travel in the open and many inquiries among other refugees they were helping, he found us, while his companions continued their quest.

That night the sound of intense fighting again disturbed our sleep. It was not just unsettling noises that troubled me, however. Often I was tormented by nightmares of Manassé, drunk, trying to rape me. In the dreams I would always call on Jesus' name for deliverance.

Despite the suffering, I knew that God was drawing us closer to Himself. I was also praying for Craig and other friends abroad who I knew must be praying for me. In fact, I often sensed that Craig was praying for me, sometimes almost seeing his face etched into the mountains when I walked.

This helped during the hard days. One such day in mid-February, Mr. Ibouanga came into our family's room. "As you know I was just in Dolisie getting supplies. I'm afraid I have some bad news."

"Is Aimé all right?" Mama Jacques gasped.

"It's not Aimé. It's . . ." Mr. Ibouanga paused. "I'm sorry to bring you this news, but your home was plundered. All the doors are wide open."

Mama Jacques began to cry; the house and what was inside it represented all the family's years of hard and honest labor.

Papa Jacques interrupted. The home reflected his life savings, so his words carried special weight. "We need to praise God in all things. Let's thank our good God."

What a man of faith my father was! We had entrusted everything into God's hands, so we needed to trust that God had allowed this to happen and that He was still watching over us.

"But please don't let it be burned down," I whispered.

21

Mosquitoes in Moubotsi

Médine

Explosions sounded in the distance the next morning. Many villagers from Ngoyo, including the inhospitable toilet owner, began filing past us into Tao-tao. Ngoyo was the first village where we had found refuge. "Heavy bombing struck our village," the fugitives reported.

We knew that Tao-tao was too close to Dolisie for us to remain safe where we were, but where should we go? After praying we decided to remain in Tao-tao until we heard clear direction from the Lord.

That evening a thunderstorm flooded our shelter. "Lord, I'm thanking You for everything," I prayed with determination. Still, I remembered wistfully our comfortable beds in Dolisie. By ten that night we had cleaned out the water as best as we could. Then we laid our mats and clothes on the damp floor and tried to sleep.

Time to Go

That evening during prayer Mama Cathy saw a vision. "Take Papa Jacques to Moubotsi for now. Go to the deacon there; he'll help with lodging."

Encouraged by this word, we prepared early the next morning to leave for Moubotsi. Many people came to bid us farewell. After praying we decided to separate into two groups. Because it was not possible to navigate the wheelbarrow on the gravel alongside the railroad track, Papa Jacques would have to follow the longer and more dangerous ten-mile dirt road designed for vehicles. Pastor Nziengue's nephew, Fred, went with this group to help Emmanuel push Papa Jacques in the wheelbarrow; another man and his three wives went with that group because his vision was too poor to navigate the railroad.

Our other larger group was walking more directly along the railroad tracks. This group consisted of the rest of our family, plus the families of Pastor Nziengue and Dr. Kaya, all of us carrying bundles. I was the only one who had been to Moubotsi, so I led the way. Walking was hard for Dr. Kaya, who had had back surgery, as well as for the elderly pastor and his wife. None of us had appropriate shoes; the stones were bruising our feet.

My neck was aching from the bundle on my head and my back was sore from carrying David. Famished from lack of food, we all fought exhaustion from the scorching sun and arduous effort. Because I was walking ahead of everyone, my mind began to wander. The people behind me were dignified people now reduced to nothing. Where would we find food? Would we live or die? Where was God? Feeling hopeless, I began to cry.

Suddenly I heard someone belting out the tune for a song that goes like this: *"Tuna nunganga, tuna nunganga, mu zingolo zandi tuna nunganga."* It translates: "We will overcome, we will overcome, by His strength we will overcome."

Just as suddenly I realized that it was David singing! At that moment I felt God assuring me that whether we ate or not—indeed, whether we lived or not—God was with us. We *would* overcome.

Where to Stay?

"The railway tracks are taking too long," Dr. Kaya called out.

"There's a shortcut through the forest just ahead," I assured him. We soon descended a mountainside, gratefully drinking water at the stream and wetting our sun-scorched heads before ascending another mountainside. Finally, after walking six or seven miles, we reached the outskirts of Moubotsi in the early afternoon.

We found temporary shade under fruit trees by the Protestant church. Unfortunately the church was already swelled with refugees with no room remaining. "Where are we going to spend the night?" Thérèse wondered. The second group arrived as we were preparing our meal for the day. After the day's exertions, we were even hungrier than usual.

Dr. Kaya received welcome news. "The village has given me a room in the infirmary here. You're all welcome to stay with me."

"Let's do it," I urged. It was true that Mama Cathy had spoken a prophecy to us to stay where the deacon recommended, but he had not come back from working in the field. "We don't want to risk being stuck outside for the night if nothing else works," I added. I am normally decisive in my judgments and persuaded Emmanuel and Thérèse to join me in carrying our belongings to the infirmary. About an hour later, though, I started feeling guilty about disobeying Mama Cathy's prophecy, so Emmanuel and I waited outside in the dark under a cloud of mosquitoes.

The deacon spotted us as soon as he returned from the field. "Jacques!" he called out with pleasure upon seeing my father.

Papa Jacques had spoken at his church when he was in good health, and the deacon welcomed our family warmly. "There are rooms in the minister's house," he said. Pastor Nziengue and Mama Cathy would have one room and my parents another. The rest of us passed the night on the dirt floor of the dining room.

In many respects these were the best accommodations that we had had since leaving Dolisie. We had our own place to sleep and even roofed toilet facilities. Nevertheless the dirt dining room floor was uneven, leaving us sore after sleeping there. There was also no screen for the window, though the mosquito nets afforded some protection.

"Come back to the infirmary," Dr. Kaya invited us the next day when he heard about our poor sleep. "We have actual bamboo beds raised off the floor, though they don't have any mattresses."

The accommodations sounded wonderful at the infirmary. The only reason for the prophecy that I could imagine was that it had meant to protect us from mosquitoes. "I heard they're so thick at the infirmary that swarms covered each person there."

"Ah, that's true," Dr. Kaya admitted. "I've never seen so many mosquitoes at once in all my sixty years. But we cut the grass this morning, clearing all the area around the infirmary. There shouldn't be many mosquitoes bothering our sleep tonight."

My siblings and I moved in happily, but Dr. Kaya had been mistaken. The buzzing and biting of mosquitoes kept us longing for morning to arrive. In the early light before dawn, I noticed that David's head looked dark, as if he had grown more hair. The morning light revealed that his head was covered with mosquitoes. Most of us returned to the dirt floor for the next night.

Within a couple days, I started to feel ill effects. My head ached and I had chills and a fever, signs of malaria. One of David's eyes was swollen, perhaps from an insect bite. Some people were selling expired malaria medicine, but it was double the normal price and we could not afford to buy any. An herbal beverage that Thérèse prepared seemed to help, and I was able to lead the prayer time that afternoon. That night, however, I succumbed fully to malaria.

As I lay on the floor the next morning, a helicopter that had bombarded a nearby village flew low over ours, scattering everyone in panic. Lacking strength to flee, I could only lie there and pray. Bertheline, the nurse whose son Modé had died, had now arrived in Moubotsi and heard about my malaria. "This is the last quinine injection I have left," she offered, giving me the shot. Her act of kindness was a significant sacrifice. It was also risky. This was a reused needle, and such needles, all that many could afford, infected many Africans with HIV.

That evening at prayers a woman testified that God had answered Pastor Nziengue's prayers for her baby. By contrast, I remained sick, throwing up three times that night. I awoke the next morning exhausted and hungry.

22

Bracing Our Hearts

Médine

In contrast to Tao-tao, Moubotsi was hospitable. The local Christians were very kind, sharing whatever fruits and vegetables they could spare. We also began finding other fruits and vegetables, and could get relief from the heat by swimming in the nearby river.

Nevertheless trouble was looming. On a day in late February, the disorganized Mambas entered Moubotsi, and eleven of them gang-raped a young woman. "She's from the north," one explained. Other Mambas arrived a few hours later, trying to find those who raped the poor young woman to punish them. No one could sleep until the gunfire ended. I was getting over the malaria but was itchy all night from allergies so I did not sleep anyway.

The next morning southern soldiers poured into Moubotsi, summoning everyone to a meeting. "No one may enter or leave this village," the officer declared. "Certainly no one should try to go back to Dolisie." The next evening as we started our usual prayer meeting, gunfire erupted again. It continued for about four hours.

In the morning Thérèse and I came across a young man's body when we went to the market and we shuddered. Perhaps the heavy shelling later in the morning meant that war would end soon?

Signs of Grace

A few days later Mama Cathy prophesied to us that my father would survive the war and that I would "have a white husband with a clerical collar." She did not know that others had given such prophecies. None of them knew of my feelings for Craig. I did not know how to take these prophecies; he had not given me even a hint of interest for many years.

Mama Cathy's prophecy to us was timely. She and Pastor Nziengue had to leave unexpectedly with another one of their nephews, a southern officer, to catch transportation to their village of origin. We helped their nephew Fred to join them a day later. We would miss his help with the wheelbarrow, but we encouraged him to stay with his family.

I was feeling much better from the malaria and, during that evening's prayer meeting, was able to teach about praising God sincerely in all situations. That night I heard Thérèse prophesying in her sleep. "I, Yahweh, the Lord of hosts, I will rebuild this country." There was hope.

The present, however, remained difficult. Our feet were especially sore. Emmanuel's flip-flops broke, leaving him to hobble on railway stones with his blistered feet. We tried to fix his flip-flops with wire, though this also cut into his feet. We were subsisting on a limited supply of nearly flavorless cassava leaves and palm nuts; if this diet continued, we would eventually succumb to malnutrition. At one point I was able to purchase a few onions at a cheaper market and hoped to sell them at a different market for a little profit. When I tried to resell the onions, however, I made only 25 CFA (4¢), the same price that

I had to pay for the market taxes that allowed me to sell there. I thus remained empty-handed and discouraged.

But at this time God lifted my spirits when a man who had been away from the village pulled me aside. "Last week I dreamed that you were very ill, and God told me to pray for you," he encouraged me. That was when I had been sick with the malaria.

Guilt and Sorrow

Our situation grated on our nerves and affected our relationships. One night David, now seventeen months old, was keeping me awake with crying, and I grew angry and spanked him. After a while he fell asleep, but I could not sleep. I lay there contemplating my behavior. Maybe David was crying because he was hungry; we had not eaten since four o'clock. Maybe he was crying because of the mosquitoes biting his feet. Whatever the reason, I asked the Lord to forgive me and help me to be a good mother. The next day I took David to the river and began teaching him to swim.

Sadly, the children were now playing war all the time, revealing the struggles that dominated their thoughts. Even little David pretended to be a soldier.

One night Emmanuel and I received heartbreaking news from some travelers. First we learned that Angolan soldiers were advancing toward this village, Mafoubou.

Second was a message sent to my father from Sous-off, whom I had not seen since I had heard him telling Zonzon of his plans to return to Dolisie. "Tell Mousounga Jacques that he must go on to Mossendjo now," one of the men said. "Sous-off says that his house has now been not only ransacked but burned."

Emmanuel and I were speechless, past tears. Our family had lost almost everything of physical value.

"How do we tell our parents?" I asked. "We dare not raise Papa Jacques's blood pressure."

Emmanuel nodded solemnly as we went inside the minister's house where we were staying. "You know, in times like these," he said to them simply, "we need to brace our hearts. Something could well happen to our house and belongings."

Death Train

The next day gunshots pierced the air. Most evenings the village crier would march through the village shouting various messages. Usually his message was, "Fathers, mothers, if the village is bad it will be your fault," so that we refugees nicknamed him affectionately "The Village Is Bad." This day, however, he was summoning able-bodied men. "You must go and destroy the bridge near Tao-tao tomorrow," he told them. "You must cut off the train line." It was clear that trouble was heading our way.

Emmanuel went fishing early the next morning. Instead of heading for the market as usual, I set apart more time to pray. "You hold everything in Your hands," I prayed. "If we die, we'll be with You." That put our situation in a larger perspective.

Around four that afternoon, panic broke out in the village. The southerners who had gone to Tao-tao to cut the rails were running back. "Angolan tanks are already in Tao-tao!" they shouted.

What had we done, staying in this village? And what could we do now? We could not leave. Emmanuel had not returned, and we could not leave without him even had we wanted to. The villagers were fleeing into the bush or to their farms, accompanied by some of the refugees.

The deacon responsible for the minister's house came to us. "What are your plans?" he asked. "My family and I are going to spend the night in the forest." He was probably hoping not to have to come back to get the key.

155

Mama Jacques decided for us. "We're going to stay here in the minister's house until tomorrow morning," she said. Soon after this, Emmanuel returned; he had not caught many fish.

By 6:30 a.m. harsh sounds rang out.

"Gunshots," Emmanuel observed soberly.

"Yes, and the Cobras' 'death train,'" another refugee added. The railway was bringing soldiers. There was no time for further deliberation.

"Let's go!" Emmanuel shouted. He loaded Papa Jacques into the wheelbarrow, and we hurried out of the village on one of the paths toward the forest. A few minutes later a woman we knew hobbled past us with a bloody foot, injured during her flight. Few people had shoes.

The Rail Bridge

An hour later we approached some people who were stopped, crying. The "bridge" ahead of us was not even a log but just a single upside-down iron rail. This was the sort of rail used for one side of a railroad track. As we drew closer, I peered into the narrow chasm. The small river, maybe ten feet below the rail, was shallow but rapid and full of stones and tree branches. We had obviously not chosen the best path—but it was too late to turn back.

"We can't cross this," Thérèse protested. "How can we balance ourselves without falling?"

Emmanuel wasted no time. He summoned Thérèse, took her hand and—going slowly and walking sideways to have more stability—bravely led her across. Emmanuel then carried David and walked with others who were afraid.

I waited as long as possible, terrified; what if I slipped?

"Don't look at the stream," Emmanuel said, "just at me."

I did not dare look down and tried to concentrate on following Emmanuel's example. He made other trips to carry our belongings over.

Our gravest difficulties, though, awaited. How would he get Papa Jacques across? He could not push him in the wheelbarrow, and our beloved father was not a small man.

Everyone standing at the bridge held their breath as Emmanuel heaved Papa Jacques onto his back, preparing to step again onto the rail; some onlookers started cursing the president. Emmanuel was not as strong as Aimé; indeed, Emmanuel weighed less than our father. Papa Jacques could cling to his neck with only a single arm. We prayed anxiously as Emmanuel inched his way across the rail. Both breathed heavily; Papa Jacques shut his eyes. Finally they reached the other side.

But even then Emmanuel was not through.

A notably obese woman had watched frantically as Emmanuel helped Papa Jacques. "Please carry me across, too," she pleaded, crying.

Emmanuel winced. This would not be easy; but there was no time to waste. After catching his breath, he made his way back across the rail, loaded the unfortunate woman onto his back and forged ahead, once again sliding sideways one step at a time. Everyone breathed a sigh of relief when they got across.

There was one more task if we were to proceed further with Papa Jacques. Grimacing from back strain, Emmanuel again made his way across the rail and retrieved the wheelbarrow. He was able to fix the wheel in the groove of the upside-down rail, but he could not advance sideways this time. He would have to walk straight forward, a much greater challenge to his balance. Sweat poured over his aching body with each uncertain and painful step. Finally he reached us. We all helped Papa Jacques into the wheelbarrow, and Emmanuel began pushing again. I could see the fierce agony piercing his back.

We were not alone on our journey. Swarming along many different trails nearly everyone from Moubotsi was now fleeing. By midmorning we had crossed three rivers and stopped to rest again. The sun was beating down more intensely, and we all felt terribly thirsty. The miserable woman resting in front of me was too weak even to lower the load from her head.

Just then Yobi, the leader of the singing group at our church in Moubotsi, passed by. Yobi was a man of good humor who always made people laugh. We found that laughter was still possible even in this chaos.

But gunfire silenced us abruptly. I peered down from the top of the mountain where we were sitting. Despite my weak glasses, I could see bursts of fire and smoke from weapons. Everyone else began to move on, but I paused for a moment, struck by the awe-inspiring beauty of God's creation visible from that mountain. I almost wished I had brought my camera to capture this scene. But had I had it with me a soldier might have killed me for it at one of the checkpoints.

Emmanuel interrupted my reverie. "We need to go," he said gently.

The Dangerous Slope

An hour and a half later, as the day grew warmer, we had not yet come across any more water. Emmanuel was too thirsty to go on. Desperate, he started lapping water from puddles formed from the previous night's rain even though worms were plainly visible in them.

"Can't you wait?" I urged, motioning toward the forest ahead. The little water that I was carrying for Papa Jacques and the children was nearly gone. If we did not find water soon, we might all feel too dehydrated to continue. A nearby gunshot reminded us that continue we must.

Many paths, known to local people, led to various small villages. "Which one do we take?" I asked.

"Ma Pauline and her family left for Mbomo Center," Emmanuel suggested, noting a path marked for that village.

"Let's go there," Papa Jacques decided. As we trudged on, however, we found ourselves in a mountainous, heavy forest with large tree trunks and roots obstructing our path. To cross these obstacles, Emmanuel often had to carry Papa Jacques on his back while someone else pushed the wheelbarrow. Emmanuel was in pain and exhausted. Papa Jacques, too, was hurting; high weeds that we call razor grass were lacerating his face and arms. He could not protect himself because he needed to use his good arm to hold on to the wheelbarrow or Emmanuel's shoulder. My father was bleeding all over.

My sisters and I would run ahead; then Thérèse and I would leave David and our bags with Gracia and hurry back to try to help Emmanuel push or pull whenever Papa Jacques was in the wheelbarrow. Pushing up steep hills was particularly difficult for Emmanuel; I had not realized that Papa Jacques was so heavy—or that I could act so strong when I had to.

Eventually we reached another river, surrounded by shady fruit trees, and we refreshed ourselves there. The forest smelled damp and fresh, and the river provided a welcome reprieve before we forged ahead.

As the afternoon wore on, a chasm appeared to await us beyond the plain. The children and I were now in front, so we quickened our pace to see what lay ahead. I was wondering how we could get to the famous Mbomo from where we were. When we reached the chasm, my heart sank. We were standing atop the edge of a steep descent. The incline stretched down at a sharp angle for perhaps half a mile.

When the others arrived they started shouting in dismay.

"What kind of path is this?" Thérèse complained. "How are we supposed to cross this?"

Loose dirt, small stones and some scattered weeds and shrubs covered the steep descent, but there were no trees or anything else to hold on to. Most of us started weeping. How could we descend without sliding or falling?

Someone had to start. Wearily I strapped David firmly to my back, balanced the bundle on my head and removed my flip-flops. My flip-flops were already in bad shape, and this task would be handled better in bare feet. I turned to Praise, Lud and Nelly. "Go slowly," I urged, and followed them down the mountainside, with Gracia right behind me.

For the children it was like a game, and they reached the bottom first. Thérèse and our friend Lucie, who was carrying her son on her back, were catching up with Gracia from behind, so Gracia tried to pass me to make way for them. In the process, she bumped me, knocking me off balance. With nothing to grab hold of, I started to slide.

"Save me, God!" I cried. In that moment, horrible images flashed through my mind: landing in a thorny bush or, worse, my full weight, meager though it was, landing on David if we rolled down the hill. Somehow I managed to recover myself, trembling and sweating.

Finally at the bottom, I watched Mama Jacques making her way down behind Thérèse and Lucie. Everybody's biggest concern, of course, was the one soon voiced by Mama Jacques herself. "How can Emmanuel carry Jacques down this steep slope?" Crying, she turned away from the mountain, afraid to see her husband and son fall.

I turned to Thérèse and Lucie. "Let's leave everything here and see if we can help Emmanuel." I put David in Gracia's care, and we began struggling back up the steep ascent, slipping and sliding along the way.

Emmanuel studied the slope below for a long time, praying. He tested the ground, but before he could move ahead another refugee arrived carrying an excessive load. Since he was bare-chested, his bag had cut deeply into his skin.

"You can go ahead," Emmanuel offered. Out of respect, Emmanuel, like other Congolese, would allow older people and sick people to go first. Plus if Emmanuel lost control it would be dangerous for anyone on the path below him. Likewise, out of respect for Papa Jacques's age, other refugees coming behind now decided to wait for Emmanuel.

"Carry the wheelbarrow ahead of me," Emmanuel instructed Thérèse and Lucie. "If I slip you might be able to help break my fall. Médine, take Papa Jacques's cane and follow me. If I start to slip, grab me from behind."

That was a hopeless plan. Nevertheless, groaning again under the weight, Emmanuel heaved Papa Jacques onto his back and followed the wheelbarrow slowly down. Mama Jacques was wailing loudly.

In the middle of the slope Emmanuel's foot slipped.

Papa Jacques could do nothing to help his son but tried to hold on. We all held our breath, praying. I could hear Emmanuel panting and could see him sweating. Somehow he managed to regain his balance. After several more tense minutes, Emmanuel brought our father safely to the ground. We all thanked God.

Mbomo Center

It was already dark when the village itself came into sight. Before we could enter it, however, we encountered a roadblock; southern soldiers were checking travelers. "Northern spies have infiltrated the refugees," they explained.

As the soldiers rummaged through our bags they discovered that everyone in the group had Bibles. "Even God's children are suffering," one of the soldiers noted sympathetically.

Once through the checkpoint we waited as Emmanuel arrived last of all, wearily pushing Papa Jacques in the wheelbarrow. One of the soldiers approached him, raising our anxiety.

For long moments the man stood looking at Emmanuel. "My brother," he intoned softly, "I admire what you're doing for your father. I don't think I would have had the courage to do such a thing." With his encouragement ringing in our ears, we dragged ourselves into the village. There was no infirmary or Protestant church in Mbomo Center, so we proceeded directly to the elementary school. Like most village schools, it had a blackboard on the wall, wooden benches and dirt floors but no fans and just large openings for windows.

As we made our way toward the classrooms, it grew obvious that the school was already full. Our hearts sank; we had arrived too late for shelter. At that moment, however, the school's principal was exiting his house and spotted this new ragged party of refugees.

"Hey! Thérèse! Emmanuel!" he called. Principal Martin had attended school with them in Dolisie. He noticed our predicament. "Don't worry. There's an empty room left," he assured us, rummaging for the key.

We soon discovered that Doctor Mabiala's mother-in-law, Pauline, and her family, who had taken a safer path and arrived about noon, were in the two rooms next door. They had just taken in another man as well. "I believe we've met," he laughed to Emmanuel. It was the overburdened man at the top of the mountain, who introduced himself as Inspector Pi.

Exhausted though we were, mosquitoes and aches inhibited our sleep once again. Even so, morning intervened too early. After sunrise we learned that the village barely had even a market. The only river here was one that wound around the village like a snake; water dropped over a high waterfall, forming something like a flowing lake at the bottom. We waded into the lake to fetch water. After we returned to our room we discovered that, among many local superstitions and prohibitions, no one was allowed to go inside the lake—as we had just done.

"What sort of superstitious village is this?" I wondered. By the next morning, however, we all found ourselves itching because of the water.

News swiftly arrived that northern soldiers had plundered the hospitable village of Moubotsi. Because the villagers had fled before soldiers arrived, however, Moubotsi had fared better than the Wicked Village, Tao-tao. Other villages on the main roads were also attacked.

"We're stuck," Emmanuel said. "It's too dangerous to travel on right now."

During the prayer time that evening, Principal Martin and his family, along with Mr. Pi's wife and daughter, joined us. We discussed Exodus 23:20–25, how God sent His angel before Israel when leading them and protected them from sickness. That night, however, David's temperature rose high again.

After worshiping on Sunday morning, Emmanuel and I hiked with some other refugees over to a little village near us. Women did most buying and traveling on the roads because soldiers randomly stopped and executed able-bodied men without any good reason. Nevertheless dear Emmanuel insisted on coming. "Médine, you know I'd give my life to keep you safe," he said. Women traveling were periodically raped. Rape was a frequent weapon of war, and often in Congo, tragically, husbands, sometimes even pastors, rejected their wives who had been raped. The trip to the village was uneventful, but because it was growing late we decided to return by a shorter route through nearby villages instead of moving along the rail line.

As we were crossing a road, a soldier on duty at a checkpoint summoned us over. Since he was from the south, we were hopeful there would not be trouble. Unfortunately the red-eyed guard was obviously high on drugs, and he started threatening Emmanuel.

"What are you doing out here, Crazy Man?" he shouted at Emmanuel. "You can't hide from us! I ought to shoot you right now." He fixed his gun on Emmanuel's head. Southern soldiers had been hunting a man from Dolisie whom they had nicknamed *"Guy le Dingue"* ("Guy the Crazy Man"), suspecting him of supporting the north.

"You've got the wrong person!" I screamed desperately. Others pleaded, but the guard would not back down. He continued shouting, his gun remaining fixed on Emmanuel's head. Emmanuel could only whisper a desperate prayer.

Finally a higher officer who had been watching the scene marched up to the shelter. "Just stop it now." He reprimanded the soldier sharply. "This is obviously not *Guy le Dingue.*" The subordinate lowered his gun from Emmanuel's head.

"You all move on," the officer commanded.

I was trembling as we left; close calls came too often.

Soon Lucie and I were pounding cassava leaves to prepare them for cooking when Lucie spotted a locust's legs in the bowl before her. She looked sick. "We must have pounded locusts into the food."

I winced. "If we throw it out, there'll be no meal today."

Lucie shrugged with disgust. "If we cook them, we'd better not tell anyone."

Everyone ate the meal gratefully that evening, but Lucie and I ate it only with difficulty, knowing what gave the cassava leaves their special taste.

23

Zonzon's Return

War had dragged on in Dolisie now for more than two months; most of that time we had spent in small villages. Everything was about to change dramatically. Very early one morning we heard a military vehicle outside.

"Where is Moussounga Jacques?"

We recognized Zonzon's voice. He had evidently learned that his property-owning uncle was in Mbomo Center. We rose with panic and glanced at one another.

I whispered, "I don't want to go stay with a family that doesn't like us." We had never told Papa Jacques how badly we had been treated by several particular relatives in his hometown of Mossendjo.

But there was no time to come up with a plan. Principal Martin, wakened at this early hour, had already opened his door. "Moussounga Jacques is staying over there," he explained graciously. The principal had no way of knowing that we might wish more time to prepare. Supporting himself on his cane, Papa Jacques met Zonzon at the door.

"I've come to get you at great risk. Now prepare your belongings and get ready to go," Zonzon ordered. Then he stepped outside, waiting. Emmanuel, Thérèse and I gathered close to one another to discuss the matter quickly.

"You remember the prophecy," Thérèse warned. "Danger awaits our father in Mossendjo." But we realized that ultimately the decision was not ours.

We joined Papa Jacques. "What do you think?" Emmanuel asked him.

"I still own a dilapidated dwelling there," he noted soberly. "Perhaps the Lord is now leading me there." Because of Papa Jacques's good job with the railroad, he had been able to purchase property. In a setting lacking insurance, it was a prudent way to invest in a family's future. "But you don't have to come," he added. "You must decide for yourselves."

We conferred again quickly. "If we let our parents go to Mossendjo alone," Thérèse warned, "they might be mistreated and even die."

"We need to stay together," Emmanuel decided. "If Papa Jacques insists on going to Mossendjo, we're going with him." We prepared our few belongings. Mr. Pi, Principal Martin and others helped us. After quick goodbyes, at around three a.m., all eleven of us (plus the driver) squeezed tightly into the military vehicle—with the wheelbarrow tied on top—and traveled through the short remainder of the night.

After riding for about two hours, we stopped to rest in the courtyard of a Catholic church in Makabana; from here we would have to find other transportation to Mossendjo.

"So why were you hesitating to come earlier?" Zonzon confronted Emmanuel.

"It just took us a while to get our things together," Emmanuel answered, trying to avoid a quarrel. After a few minutes of such discussion, nine-year-old Lud diverted our attention. "I saw an angel in front of the car gesturing as if to say, 'Come.'"

An angel was going on before the car, just like in the passage from Exodus we had read recently.

"God will help us," Papa Jacques reminded us.

Flavien's Truck

Transport vehicles started arriving in the market by mid-morning. Zonzon had enough money only for his own ticket, and we had barely any money left. As I was pacing back and forth anxiously, with David strapped to my back, a soldier approached.

"Marie!"

"Greetings," I answered politely. "It's Médine."

"Yes, yes, sorry." He realized from my response that I did not recognize him, but he did not seem to mind. "It's Flavien. Flavien Ngada. I see you're looking for a ride. You should board my vehicle when you're ready."

I raised an eyebrow. "I'm not alone," I replied. "I have my family with me, and we might not have enough money for our fares." I pointed them out.

"I'm going to help you," Flavien announced generously. He was a wild soldier, but could be kind to those he liked. "Your parents and the three children won't have to pay anything." Because David was on my back or in my arms the whole time, he was already exempt. "So just get tickets for yourself, your two sisters and your brother, and you can board."

I was stunned and went to announce this turn of events to the family. We found that we had just enough to pay fare for the four siblings. Thanking the Lord, we boarded the crowded truck and tried to find places where we could sit.

Flavien's truck stopped often and broke down once, needing water from a river to cool the engine. It was three in the afternoon when we finally reached Mossendjo. To save time, Emmanuel, though exhausted, clambered onto the roof of the truck to untie our bags and throw them down. As he was throwing down Papa Jacques's sponge mat, he slipped. The red ground below was full of rocks.

"People get their just desserts," one bystander remarked. "That refugee survived war only to break his neck here."

Ignoring their rudeness I rushed to his side.

"I'm all right," he assured me, struggling to his feet. He had landed on Papa Jacques's sponge mat. But by the time we reached Papa Jacques's property, Emmanuel admitted to me how much his back was hurting.

Settling into Mossendjo

Although we were all sick, we were happy to be able to rest in one place for a while. Nelly was particularly happy, now reunited with her parents. No sooner had news begun to spread that Papa Jacques was in Mossendjo than many people began streaming to greet him; he had helped many people.

But while my father had been sacrificially generous, his good job had fostered jealousy in this, his hometown—and it grew conspicuous. We children had experienced this hostility for some years whenever we visited Mossendjo but had tried to shield our good-hearted father from seeing it. Now, when certain people he had helped refused to share even peanuts with him, he began to understand. He avoided discussing it, but I knew that this betrayal wounded him.

Not surprising to us, Zonzon brought a witness to Papa Jacques and tried to get Papa Jacques to let Zonzon take charge of his small pension. He also wanted Papa Jacques to let Zonzon's brother take charge of Papa Jacques's dilapidated property in Pointe-Noire—where, if he had escaped war, Eliser was presumably staying. Papa Jacques insisted, however, that he wanted to leave these things for his wife and children.

Our few rooms in the structure my father owned in Mossendjo, which were small and mostly empty, provided shelter from rain and direct sun. The only bed was in Papa Jacques's room; since it lacked a mattress, we placed the sponge mat on top of it. Everyone else laid our torn mats or body cloths on the uneven ground. (What I call a *body cloth*, a *pagne*, is a wrap a woman can use as a skirt, to tie a child on her back or to cover her at night.)

As we were gathering firewood and vegetables, some people made fun of us because we were not carrying the baskets on our backs the way the local people did. Some people also periodically laughed at Emmanuel and me.

"You went and got a Western education," they mocked. "Look, you're in rags. Your doctorates won't help you here."

Papa Jacques's health was declining significantly. I grew so discouraged that all I could do was repeat Jesus' name. One day my father called us together and instructed us, "Hope in Jesus." He turned to me since I was in charge of the food. "Médine, you should give food even to those who hate us here. Don't be sad; God is our hope." That admonition from the person who was suffering the most challenged me deeply.

Rats, Ferns and Army Ants

Although refugees who crossed over into the neighboring coastal state of Gabon had access to food and shelter in the refugee camps there, they faced risks as well: One of my close friends was brutally raped by an aid worker who was also a minister. In Mossendjo, by contrast, we had safe shelter, but food and clean drinking water were sometimes in short supply. Refugee women had nothing but rags to use as pads during their periods.

After a while children in Mossendjo began dying of starvation and malnutrition. First I would see children beginning to appear obese, then their hair would fall out, then they would have a distended stomach—and then they would die. Though better off than some others, our family was now hungry and destitute even by African standards. I forced the children to eat whether or not they liked the food. Sometimes we ate rats for protein. Nothing, though, tasted worse than ferns.

Lacking a field to grow our own food, we depended on others' charity. In contrast to the refugee camps in Gabon, no supply lines for international aid were open here yet. Sometimes Thérèse and I would leave the house early and walk six or seven miles to harvest cassava roots. The blisters on our feet often bled, and cold mountain water from the river stung like alcohol on the wounds. Snakes and disease-bearing insects posed serious dangers.

Most often, to reach the cassava fields, we had to pass through streams of army ants. Some of the ants would drop from the trees onto us; others would climb our legs. We would have to strip and pick off the ants; we could brush off the ants' bodies, killing them, but we still had to remove their mandibles from our skin. Most mornings and some evenings we also had to descend a steep mountain to fetch water, then trek back up the mountain with the full barrels or buckets on our heads. As I was malnourished, my hair and nails began to fall out.

Nevertheless war had begun to teach me that I could muster more strength, when I had to, than I imagined possible. Pulling with all our backs, we had to uproot the cassava. I normally had to lug the heavier basket because Thérèse was still frail from her prewar operation. When my back was too weak, however, Thérèse did more of the work. It felt as though we carried a hundred pounds. One day when it was raining I heard my back snap. I had to keep going, groaning every step.

You need your hands to work cassava roots. I had to peel them, sometimes cutting myself, soak them in water to get the toxins out, hand grind the cassava twice, cook it, then knead it while hot before cooking it again. One day I awoke unable to move my hands. Whenever we harvested more cassava than we could eat, we sold it, making fifty cents or a dollar a day. It was better than nothing; some famished young women were selling their bodies and contracting HIV for a piece of bread or a can of sardines.

Militias and Gangs

One day as we struggled home with baskets of cassava, we spotted the notorious Bonja Bord and members of his gang swimming in the river. He was known for using drugs and terrorizing Mossendjo. Though otherwise handsome, he was missing one hand. It had been reportedly cut off during the previous war for killing a man and seizing his wife. He had learned how to shoot and drive skillfully with one hand; meanwhile he kept the dead man's wife as his unwilling mistress. No one interfered with him.

Mossendjo was one of the centers for the southern army. People with radios reported that the northern president intended to drive the southern rebels here into the forest. Many of the southern soldiers lacked military training, fighting either because they were enthusiastic for the war or because they had no choice. Some of them were younger than sixteen. Some were children of people we knew from church.

Soon Makabana and Sibiti were bombed, and the wounded began to stream into Mossendjo for treatment. Mawa, a friend who had been with us in Moubotsi, lost his mother, his sister, nieces and nephews in the attacks. He brought one of his wounded nieces to Mossendjo's hospital.

"We saw a low-flying aircraft with an international label," he told us bitterly. "Women and children went out to meet it.

We thought the outside world was sending food or medicine. Instead, they shot us." Other victims reported that helicopters from Elf, the French oil company, had been attacking much of the south. Some claimed that they saw white people in the helicopters.

That Sunday evening we finally were rejoined by my youngest brother. After fleeing from Ngoyo, Aimé and his friends had walked more than fifty miles on a circuitous route from the bombing in Makabana to reach the relative safety of Mossendjo. He had a disturbing report. "We were eating lunch together when we saw two helicopters attacking civilians," Aimé said, "a military one and a second one marked 'Elf.' The first helicopter was firing missiles and people in the second one were shooting. I hid behind a tree."

A new local problem was brewing. Flavien Ngada, the soldier who had given my family a ride to Mossendjo, joined Bonja Bord and some other fighters to terrorize Mossendjo. They robbed the evangelical parish of Madouma; Pastor Massamba escaped, telling me that God enabled him to walk unseen past his assailants.

Then Bonja Bord and his gang invaded a bar and killed two soldiers from Sibiti. In retaliation, soldiers from Sibiti's militia started terrorizing Mossendjo, taking the law into their hands.

"We're looking for Bonja Bord and his gang," they insisted, but in the process they also burned the city treasury. The soldiers from Sibiti ambushed and killed Flavien. Despite the bad things I heard about him, I could not forget the kindness he had shown me.

Before the month ended, soldiers captured Bonja Bord, burned him alive and freed the young widow he had kept captive. I avoided the execution, but because the site was part of my neighborhood, it smelled like burnt flesh there that day. Early the next morning, as I was on my way to the market, I encountered dogs eating some of his remains and I nearly threw up.

Falling Sick

There was never enough food for all of us. Aimé's friends would come to eat with us, and I could apportion the food only with difficulty. I continued to give priority to my parents and the children. We always felt hungry. We began falling sick one after the other.

That is why I was often sick with malaria or other illnesses. Medicine was more available in Mossendjo than in the other locations where we had stayed, but we could not afford it. During the dry season, we often shivered at night because we lacked blankets. Moreover we still had only flip-flops, not real shoes. One day Emmanuel went fishing with a makeshift pole and punctured his foot on a massive thorn. We cleaned his wound but had no disinfectant. Since we lacked toilet paper, we mostly used leaves. Some began to suffer bloody hemorrhoids. On one occasion it appeared that Emmanuel's bowels were protruding from his rectum; he was able to reinsert them only with much agony.

Papa Jacques was speaking with difficulty now, taking a long time to get out even a word. Had he experienced another stroke? One day I was carrying heavy loads of cassava roots under a scorching sun to soak them in the Lissafi River. When I returned, I learned that he had fallen from his seat. The signs of his deterioration were now multiplying: a hesitant voice, high blood pressure and increased difficulty in walking. Yet we had no means to secure medicine, which required cash in hand.

God had blessed David, at least. Before war, a pediatrician had warned that David might need medicine for his eyes much of his life. We lacked the medicine, and David's eyes had been continually running, swollen, infected and itchy. A few weeks after Thérèse prayed for David's eyes, however, I realized that the infection had stopped. Nor had it returned.

But on the first day of July, as I was cleaning the leaves that I would use the next day to wrap the cassava bread, David was playing beside me. Abruptly he called, "Ma Médine! Ma Médine! I'm cold." I did not pay much attention, thinking he was playing a game; it was too hot out to feel cold, and David was always talkative.

"David, come over here," I called. When he did not come, I looked up. Although he had been playing just minutes earlier, he was no longer moving. He tried to talk but his voice was just a gasp, like a death rattle.

Shrieking, I dropped everything and lunged toward him. His body was cold and his feet were stiff.

I darted into Emmanuel's room. "Emmanuel! David is dying!"

24

Life and Death in Mossendjo

Emmanuel took one look at David and rushed into Papa Jacques's room. "I need the palm oil," he requested as calmly as possible.

This oil, used to massage people when they were sick, was our only medication. "What's going on?" he asked, apprehensive.

"Everything's all right," Emmanuel assured him, grabbing the oil.

Emmanuel returned, prayed for David and started massaging him. My son was very cold, and his cries were now faint. When Emmanuel finished, I strapped David to my back, and Emmanuel and I ran out to look for help. Because it was afternoon, medical personnel probably would not be available at the hospital, which lacked electricity. Moreover the hospital required payment up front, and we did not have money.

So we dashed off to find Emmanuel's friend Clément. Clément was not technically a doctor but he had a degree in medicine. He ran a private clinic and was the most competent help available. As we were running, Emmanuel kept calling David: "David-o, David-o, are you all right?" David was still answering faintly, but I could not feel him move on my back.

I was too overwhelmed to know what to think or how to pray. All I could do was keep repeating, "Father God, help us." Finally my prayer became more focused. "Oh, God, let us find Doctor Clément." He could be visiting family or in the fields looking for food since he did not have many patients yet.

When we reached his clinic, however, he was inside. As soon as he saw David and listened to Emmanuel's explanation, his eyes widened. "You're lucky—I have just one injection left." David uttered muffled cries as he received the injection. "Put him on the bed," Clément directed. "Now that he's got the medicine he'll warm up in few minutes." After five or ten minutes, David started to move; his cries grew stronger and his body was warm.

"I know you'll need payment immediately," I started to apologize.

"Just pay me when you get the money," Clément assured us graciously. "For now, take the child to the Massimbas' private lab and get him a malaria test."

As soon as we left the office, David started asking questions again, incessantly as usual. "Talk as much as you want," I assured him, weeping tears of relief and gratitude. Emmanuel collected whatever money we had available to pay Clément.

The next day Gracia and I went again with our friend Blaise to the cassava field belonging to his mother. Army ants were swarming the soil and the trees. God had once spoken to me about tests of faith being like getting through fields of army ants; it is difficult, but one can get to the other side. This day, in seeking to evade the ants, Gracia, Blaise and I each fell and got hurt.

But others were suffering more. On returning home, exhausted, I learned that Zonzon's nephew Adam was now in a coma in the hospital with malaria. In contrast to David, he did not recover; he died the next morning.

War and Peace

A couple of days later I began to overhear more news of the war. Angolan soldiers were advancing toward Mossendjo! Local southern militias banded together, and the Angolans, who had raped and plundered Makabana's civilians, fled as they heard the troops advancing. But some of the undisciplined southern soldiers began plundering their own people in areas that the Angolan soldiers had missed. War dulls people's moral sensibilities, and civilians make easy targets for both sides.

One southern soldier killed about this time was Sous-off, who had sent word that Papa Jacques's home in Dolisie was destroyed. One day Nelly had met him in Mossendjo and asked him, "How did you find out that Papa Jacques's home was destroyed?"

Nelly told us later that he had stammered an answer, avoiding the question. His secret would now rest with him.

For those of us who survived, life continued as usual. Because my French was so proficient, I preached in the French services periodically for Mossendjo's evangelical church, preaching especially that people would have eternal life if they trusted Christ. Because crowds gathered when I spoke, the pastor often invited me. Still, I felt too embarrassed by my flip-flops and tattered clothes—my only garment—to sit on the designated chair. Our flip-flops seemed to break whenever we walked in mud.

Yet people shared words of hope with me. A pastor prophesied, "You'll go overseas someday." Another refugee prophesied that I would go to the U.S. "And I see you and David being called American," she added. A few months later a woman of prayer declared, "You're the Lord's servant, and you should go back to teaching youth. And also, God has prepared a husband for you." I often felt the strong urge to write to Craig, but I would not know where to send a letter: My address book was gone forever, left behind in the home that burned.

Snakes and God's Provision

Papa Jacques usually sat in his house facing the window, praying, reading the Bible or thinking, except when people would visit him. One late afternoon, he spotted a massive lethal snake, probably ten feet long, slithering through the doorway. He could not protect himself. "Antoinette! Antoinette!" he began calling.

His speech was not always understandable at this time, but Mama Jacques, who was outside, heard the alarm in his voice. Hurrying to him, she saw the snake draped across the doorway—but the machete she needed to kill it was inside the house. Besides that, she was afraid of snakes! But as the snake moved behind some large jars, she rushed inside and seized the machete.

God, I don't know what I'm doing. Please help me! she prayed, and started striking the floor behind the containers, sometimes with her eyes closed. It was now getting dark, so she could not see what she was striking. After she had been striking blows for a while, she moved a container and was relieved to spot pieces of the snake. But then she noticed that the head was still alive, looking for something to strike. Her final blow split its skull.

The danger past, my father returned to his prayer vigil. "Since prayer is all that I'm able to do, it's my contribution for the family right now," he promised. It was no small contribution.

Thérèse and I often had to wade through water to get to food, and our father prayed for our safety. One time when I prayed with a certain woman she had a vision. "I see you walking through muddy water that you can't see through to get to a cassava field. Is this true?"

"Yes," I confirmed.

"I see snakes in the water, but God protects you as you walk."

Cassava grows less during the dry season. By early September we were fasting and praying intensely; we were on the brink of begging for food or literally starving. Two-year-old David experienced another malaria attack and went into convulsions. Later in the month his ears were expelling pus. Yet medicine was hard to come by, and war kept dragging on.

We devoted the next few days to concerted prayer again, concluding with a fast. Having lived for a year as refugees, we felt somehow that God was at work. That evening a traveler just come from Gabon brought Emmanuel word that a parcel was waiting for him at Congo's border with Gabon. What could it be? There was only one way to find out. Emmanuel borrowed some money for his ticket to take a truck early the next morning. We prayed anxiously; soldiers controlled trucks heading to the border.

The next evening he returned. We flooded him with questions, but he simply grinned until the guests were gone and then gathered us in Papa Jacques's room. Opening his bag he pulled out real soap, a treasured commodity that we had not seen for a long time. He then pulled out some cookies for the children; Praise and Lud grasped their treats excitedly. Finally he pulled out a huge pile of cash.

We were all too shocked to speak. I started to cry. We had been feeding twelve to fourteen people on about fifty cents a day, and our money was almost gone again. Now we realized that we would not starve.

Mama Jacques raised everyone's question: "What happened?"

Emmanuel smiled. "When my friends in France heard about our country's war, they took up an offering—more than six hundred dollars. Then when our cousin Leopold visited France they gave it to him; he gave it to a visiting relative who's staying among the refugees in Gabon. We're close to the border. . . ."

Knowing the future, God had set the answer to our prayer in motion before we had even prayed it.

"Many travelers have been killed for less than fifty dollars," Emmanuel added. "And despite all the hands it passed through, not a cent is missing." We praised God together, greatly encouraged.

Bamboo Assailants

We used a significant part of our money to buy medicine for Papa Jacques, trying to conserve the rest of it wisely given how many mouths we were feeding. There was no way to predict when the war would end. We thus continued working the cassava fields and sewing up our tattered underwear. Rainy season arrived and the roof often leaked on us. Worst of all was how the war conditions affected our relationships. Sometimes we got upset with each other over a piece of bread or fruit.

One night in October we heard a sound like gunfire. "The Cobras are attacking!" some shouted. People began throwing together their valuables and loading them on their backs or heads. Many rushed into the forest to spend the night.

"What are you going to do?" a neighbor asked, preparing to leave.

"We're staying put until we get news from the soldiers who went to check," Emmanuel told him.

Deep in the night, the soldiers returned and assured everyone through a loudspeaker that it was nothing. In the morning we learned that the "gunshots" were bamboos that caught fire and were rattling out under the heat. General anxiety had people primed for panic, and it had not come without a price. Some of the fugitives in the forest were killed by snakes.

"Life is hard," I wrote in my journal in November, "but Jesus is everything to me." I trusted that His promises would come to pass. I was now almost 36 years old, and though I longed to marry and have more children, time was running out.

One morning, when I was cooking cassava in our aunt's kitchen, Emmanuel burst in. "Médine . . . I'm sorry. The Resistance has summoned you." I stared at him unmoving. "They have captured a spy—and want you to translate for them."

25

The Outside World

Entering the designated house warily, I found two men waiting.

"You recognize Samuel Malonga, of course," one man remarked, gesturing to the other. Because I had never had a television I did not recognize him, but I knew his name: He was a famous television journalist. "You need to follow him to the checkpoint. There we need you to interpret for a captured spy who can't speak French."

At the checkpoint I found myself facing a frighteningly large, robust man with visible bruises. "You will sit by him and translate our questions and his answers," a soldier instructed.

I felt blood rush to my face. This man was too big! "I'm sorry, but there's no way I'm going to sit by him," I said. "If he loses his temper, he could crush me."

"I'll sit between you," Samuel Malonga agreed. The journalist and I worked from 10:00 a.m. to 5:30 p.m.

"I'm just a businessman on a trip to Gabon," the captured young man insisted in English. His name was Mustafa

Aboubacar from Sierra Leone. "I know nothing of Sassou," he said of the current president.

"This is false," an interrogator snapped. "The Gabonese police handed you over to us because you tried to fly over Mossendjo. You are a spy." And so it continued until, exhausted, I was able to leave. The Resistance paid me for my efforts. The next day local radio aired parts of the interview, but after that a more eager translator took my place. That arrangement was more than fine with me; I did not want this job!

Truce!

By mid-December planes were flying above Mossendjo at low altitude, but so far God had been protecting this refugee town. We were all just barely surviving; I looked like skin draped over bones.

On Christmas Eve northern aircraft bombed Makabana again, and everyone expected Mossendjo to be next. That night, starting at midnight, we held an all-night prayer vigil, which we repeated on New Year's Eve. Many refugees joined us, as well as the church youth group that Aimé now led.

"God is going to give you a husband," Aimé prophesied to me that night. "You'll see your friends overseas, and someday you'll travel much for the Lord." At midnight we danced and praised God joyfully for seeing us safely into the New Year.

On January 11, 2000, we learned that a peace treaty was finally signed, and Mossendjo was jubilant. "We signed the peace treaty," Colonel Boungouanza announced, "because civilians are suffering. We're making peace now. Soldiers, go back to your villages."

War was over.

Our lives, however, remained difficult. We would soon be out of money again because of the many needs, such as purchasing malaria medicine for those both inside and outside the family. But after we had lived for a year and a half on the run, time had come to reestablish contact with the outside world. In early February, Emmanuel left for Pointe-Noire, the one city that had been spared war and where we hoped to find my other brother Eliser.

"Please try to find addresses for my friends," I urged. "Especially Craig."

The same day, Mustafa, the alleged spy from Sierra Leone, saw me selling bananas on the road in front of our dwelling. "I haven't eaten for two days," he pleaded. "After your people beat me and seized everything I had, they let me go. But I have no food."

I paused. I had shared what we had with displaced civilians from the north, but no one thought that Mustafa was a civilian. People still believed that he had come to bomb Mossendjo. Moreover we had little ourselves. But Jesus taught that we should love everyone.

"Come in," I invited, and served him food. From then on he often ate with us until he found another means of support.

Meanwhile news got around that our home in Dolisie had been burned. But rather than show sympathy, many people ridiculed us. None of us had anything to show for our years of hard work and prayer. We did not even have money to transport the family back to Dolisie. Papa Jacques saw my discouragement. "Let's praise God for what we've become," he offered.

"I'm learning how to live in poverty, trusting God," I wrote in my journal. "I hope that one day when I have enough again to eat and wear, I won't forget what I've learned."

The Soldier's Windshield

When Emmanuel returned, the news he gave us about his trip was mixed. On the train to Pointe-Noire, Emmanuel witnessed soldiers extorting money or goods from travelers emerging from war. Soldiers stripped women and publicly searched their private parts to make sure that they were not hiding valuables; some women were raped. One soldier slashed a woman's thigh because she did not hand over fifty cents quickly enough. But the soldiers were armed and no one could stop them.

Positively, in Pointe-Noire Emmanuel quickly located Eliser. The only family member not displaced by war, Eliser had carried a different burden. "Everyone was telling me that Papa Jacques died. I couldn't believe it in my heart." He had also heard that I died. Emmanuel happily dispelled the rumors.

Emmanuel further told us how, after leaving Eliser, he traveled on by train to Dolisie. He watched nervously as a Cobra, apparently high on drugs, boarded the car, dragging an expensive, stolen windshield that he hoped to sell.

"I'm leaving my windshield right here for now," the soldier warned. "If anyone so much as *touches* it, I'll kill you." Emmanuel was uncomfortable to have the fragile object behind him. He breathed a sigh of relief when the soldier departed for another car.

It was very hot, the train was overcrowded and Emmanuel had malaria. After he finished taking his medicine, when he was returning his water bottle into his pack, the train began grinding to a halt at a village stop. As the train and its passengers lurched back and forth, Emmanuel's water bottle slipped and smashed against the hot windshield, cracking it.

Returning to this car, the Cobra immediately noticed the state of his precious glass plate.

"Who smashed my windshield?" he demanded furiously. Everyone remained silent.

The Cobra drew his firearm, determined to exact vengeance. He pointed it at a man near Emmanuel. "Tell me! Who did it? You? Or someone else?" Emmanuel was praying silently, fearing that he would never again see his parents to say goodbye.

Another Cobra intervened. "Look, the sun is hot. Don't you know that the sun's heat can break the glass?"

The first Cobra heaved his shoulders angrily and marched off the train car.

"Thank You, Lord," Emmanuel whispered, "for sparing my life again."

Safe Amid the Ruins

Finally Emmanuel reported to us what he had seen in our home city. "It's true," Emmanuel said. "Our house in Dolisie was destroyed." He told us that when he had surveyed the ruins of our home in Dolisie, he had begun weeping. Everything inside had been either plundered or burned. He wept especially for Papa Jacques, who had invested in this home almost everything that he did not give away. After praying, Emmanuel found the strength to forgive our enemies.

"But it's strange," he added. "It didn't look like the work of Cobras or Angolan soldiers." No one had stolen my crock-pot or the porcelain dishes my church in France had given me; no one had stolen Emmanuel's car. Instead, these things were set aside and burned—as if someone just wanted to intensify our suffering.

"More tellingly," Emmanuel continued, "a man told me that he had overheard soldiers speaking Kitsangui when the home was plundered and burned." Kitsangui was the language of Mossendjo. "A southern soldier also apologized to me about the house, saying that he wasn't one of the ones involved." In any case, furniture, family photos—all of our possessions were gone.

"Remember Job's example," Papa Jacques urged. "Let's praise God."

"One piece of good news," Emmanuel added. "You didn't find my documents before you fled. But outside my room I saw a pile of dark ashes wet from rain. Whoever did this had piled our papers and other things to burn them there. Deep inside the pile we found a folder in a plastic bag. It contained my diplomas—unharmed. Maybe the Lord wants me to have employment someday!"

Aid and Corruption

Conditions began improving. I now had a toothbrush; for a year, I had been using roots to clean my teeth. With supply lines open, international aid began pouring in. Especially active in Mossendjo were Doctors Without Borders and the International Red Cross. One day aid workers arrived to clean a well from which we had been drawing water for months. As I watched, they removed babies' diapers, feminine pads, underwear and the like. I felt nauseous; it was no wonder my mother had contracted typhoid. We had also been suffering dysentery, drinking from rivers polluted with human waste and other debris; malnutrition had weakened our immune systems. But we had to have water.

I translated some English letters that arrived with international aid. One was from an English girl. "I'm using all my allowance to provide this gift for a child in Congo," she wrote. As I translated the letter, I was so overwhelmed by the kindness of this young outsider that I started crying. Unfortunately some well-off local people who were chosen to distribute supplies kept some of the best things for themselves. Still, most goods, especially for children, and food such as rice and lentils got through.

I had been teaching the teenagers' Sunday school class at church. The young people expressed their love for me by calling me "Big sister" or "Mother." One Sunday I encouraged them to bring their needs to God in prayer. Nearly twenty were present at that time. After they recounted their needs we prayed together.

At the end a student asked, "Big Sister, what should we pray for you?"

My eyes dropped down to my gaunt body, clothed with rags. "Let's ask God to give me something to wear. Otherwise I'll be completely naked soon."

No sooner had we closed with that prayer and walked out of the building than someone caught up with me and grabbed my hand. It was the mother of a friend who was abroad.

"Médine, come to my house," she said with a smile.

Once inside she handed me an old plastic bag. "This is for you," she offered simply. Inside I found the most beautiful fabric I had seen for a long time. I could make some clothes for myself, David and others.

"Thank you, thank you!" I stammered, tears forming in my eyes. I hurried back to the church. Some of the youth were still there, talking, and I showed them the fabric. God had answered our prayer right away.

The Craig Who Writes Books

At the end of May, I was pondering again the many prophecies given me regarding marriage, and those thoughts always led to Craig. I wanted to try to let him know I was safe. Emmanuel began the process for me by locating a friend in France.

"Try to find how to contact the Craig Keener who writes books," he pleaded for me in a letter.

Craig

Almost every day as I checked my mailbox, I looked in vain for a letter from Médine telling me that she was safe. No matter what else I found there, I was always disappointed. I kept asking Francophone Africans about the Congo, considering traveling there to look for her.

"You don't know the local languages or politics," they warned. "You won't help your friend by getting killed."

Médine

Emmanuel and I have loyal friends, and not one in the chain of communication failed. His African friend in France was able to obtain Craig's phone number. This friend then contacted his fiancée's mother, who lived in the States. She reached Craig and asked for his email address. That African friend then called Eliser's pastor in Pointe-Noire, asking him to pass it on; Eliser happened to be present in the pastor's office at that very moment. Eliser relayed the email address to Emmanuel, who then asked another friend in France, Serge, to contact Craig and let him know I was alive.

Craig

My heart jumped that day when my phone rang and a polite woman said that her daughter's fiancé in France wanted my email address for someone in Africa.

"For Médine?" I asked. Knowing that if she escaped Dolisie alive she would not have my address, I had always prayed that she could locate me through my books.

The woman did not know, but I gave her the address just in case—and then heard nothing for many more days.

At long last I received the email message from Serge: "Your friend Médine is alive," he wrote. Though I was elated by that information, the rest of the message scared me. "But she's in the forest, with no access to food or medicine." I did not understand that *in the forest* could include villages within the rainforest.

I was on my way to Nigeria for the summer but wrote back, pleading with Serge to let me know what I could do. Meanwhile my friends in Nigeria had taken on the mission of looking for a wife for me there. One woman I met was doing great work for the Lord, but when she stepped out of the room for a moment, her friend, known as a prophetess, turned to me quickly. "This is not your future wife," she informed me. "But don't worry— you'll be meeting your future wife in the spring."

My eyebrows lifted. "Spring as in literally this coming year? Or figuratively as in when my time of waiting is over?"

She shrugged. "I don't know."

I hated ambiguous prophecies.

Just before I had met Médine, some people had prophesied that I would meet my wife "soon." After a while I took that vague prediction with a grain of salt. The subjectivity of some immature charismatic prophecy embarrassed me, though I also knew the reality of the Spirit's activity.

Still, I took comfort. And I wondered—maybe I would soon hear from Médine? I spent the private hours I had over the next few days weeping in prayer for both of us—for Médine's safety and for my heart to be pure before the Lord.

"Lord, I'll continue to remain single if that pleases You," I prayed. "I'll continue to keep my heart pure from lust before You. These years of loneliness are draining my strength. But I love You more. I won't knowingly step outside your will."

Returning to Philadelphia, I reaffirmed my trust in God to guide me in His time. In moments of weaker faith, I wondered about the letter someone had sent me a decade earlier, claiming that Cass's abandoning me and the loss of my marriage were God's judgment against me. I dealt with such fears and loneliness the only way I knew—I buried myself again in my intensely disciplined schedule of writing, teaching and ministering to others, while the hollow part of my soul sank deeper and deeper.

I was headed for collapse.

26

Out of the Forest

Médine

Our money was nearly gone; we resolved, however, that the children should return to school, requiring fees. The family prayed for me, and I set out with Emmanuel for Pointe-Noire to look for work. From there I also hoped to contact Craig. With great anguish, I had to leave beloved David behind with my family for safety's sake.

Postwar Travel

Emmanuel and I stood in the crowded open back of a truck, like sardines packed in a can, clinging to an iron rail. Part of a wheel on the truck was broken, but the driver decided it was good enough. At Makabana, he decided that he did not want to stop at the security checkpoint where he would have to pay a dollar. Thus he sped up and kept driving fast; five or six miles from the next town, however, we started screaming for him to stop.

The truck ground to a halt. "What are you yelling about?" he called back, agitated. As he stopped, the wobbly tire fell off completely. Riding a different truck from Makabana to Dolisie, we were searched at every checkpoint.

In Dolisie only briefly, I quickly found Mama Jeanne, known for her prayers. "You nearly had an accident on the way here," she prophesied, "but God protected everyone on your vehicle because of you both. As for Papa Jacques: Some of his relatives think he has a lot of money, and they don't want his children being the ones to benefit from it. But God will bring him back alive to Dolisie. You should make plans to return to Dolisie—just don't let it be known to those who might wish to prevent it."

Emmanuel and I caught a ride on an open lumber train full of soldiers; we clambered onto the large logs. As the train advanced we looked solemnly as ghost towns, once teeming with life, passed before us.

Finally, in Pointe-Noire, I saw Eliser for the first time in a year and a half; he was emaciated. "I've been ill," he explained.

That night I dreamed about Craig. In the dream Craig drew on his own experience with divorce to help me legally ratify the end of my bigamous situation. I had filed for divorce before the war and had believed that it was finished, but because the law office was burned, I had to pay again.

"Thank You, God," I affirmed when I awoke. When I had first met Craig, I could not understand why a man of God would be so sad. Now I understood the anguish of a broken marriage, though my situation was different. He did not want his divorce; I needed one.

Finally in a city with a functioning mail system, I was able to write to Craig. I could not afford to send email, so I sent a letter, praying that it would reach him.

Return with Eliser

After a week in Pointe-Noire, Emmanuel stayed behind while I started back to Mossendjo with Eliser, who had not seen our parents since Dolisie's fall. As we prepared to board another cargo train, soldiers were searching all large bags. A soldier jerked out some clothes I had bought for David. "You're going to sell these. You need to pay me duties."

"How could I sell two pairs of clothes?" I protested indignantly. "I shouldn't have to pay."

At that moment someone who knew me greeted me, and the soldier, perhaps uncomfortable with having a witness to his behavior, grimaced. "Go on, get out of here."

As the train lurched forward, I noticed an emaciated, middle-aged woman sitting nearby. She was trying to reach her family, but after we had traveled about twenty miles, she died. Her relative did not dare cry because he would be charged an extra fee for transporting a corpse. As soon as the train reached Bilinga, however, he dragged the body off the train and laid it on the stony soil. He and the relatives waiting for them began to sob.

After Mvouti, Eliser and I mounted yet another cargo train. Northern soldiers extorted travelers on the passenger trains that ran the safer route; many thus preferred to ride these more dangerous, open wagons. From Les Bandas we boarded a passenger truck headed for Dolisie. Maybe forty of us crowded onto it, including some on top. Every time the truck turned, we were all pinned tightly against each other, and children cried because it was hard for them to breathe. Some three miles from Dolisie, the truck broke down with two flat tires, leaving us all to walk the rest of the way into town.

The next day I finally walked around my city. Dolisie had been badly damaged, and many homes had been destroyed. I had mixed emotions as we examined the ruins of our home. The main home was indeed destroyed, but the quarters beside it, where my brothers had stayed, looked salvageable. "God can 'rebuild the ancient ruins,'" Eliser observed hopefully.

When Mama Suzanne heard that we were in Dolisie, she came and spoke prophetically to us: "Papa Jacques must come back to Dolisie with all his family."

We reached Mossendjo late the next night, and Papa Jacques was eager to tell me something. "I heard a voice in a dream," he said. "Three times it declared that you were freed." I asked Papa Jacques the date of the dream and realized that it came one night after I had dreamed about Craig helping me get free from Manassé. Surely something was beginning to happen.

"Three years have been long enough to wait for Manassé to show up. And," my father added with a big smile, "God will give you a good husband, because He told me so in a dream before the war."

Craig

Every day I prayed as I checked my mail, hoping for word from Médine. One day in early August, I was chatting with a visitor when I opened my seminary mailbox and spotted a letter from Congo with distinctive handwriting.

"Excuse me for a moment," I explained to my guest, my heart pounding wildly. "I've been waiting a year and a half for this letter."

I tore it open right away.

"I'm alive!" it began triumphantly. "I, Médine Moussounga, am alive!"

Moments later Kristin Frederich, our dean of student spiritual formation, walked by to find me dancing. I had asked many people to pray for Médine, but Kristin was one of the few in whom I had confided my deep feelings concerning her. She was thrilled by the good news. That night I testified before a couple thousand people at Enon, my church, what God had done.

I tried to contact Médine by return mail, seeking ways to get funds to her. "Since your letter a year and a half ago," I wrote, "I've prayed every day for your safety. Sometimes I was so anxious that even while asleep I dreamed about meeting you in hiding in the Congo."

I began once more the anxious checking of my mailbox, but no reply came.

Médine

I shared with my family the prophecies that Mama Jeanne and Mama Suzanne had spoken about Papa Jacques returning to Dolisie. A few days later, Papa Jacques dreamed that Coco Moïse was urging him to return to Dolisie. Often Papa Jacques heard a voice in his dreams warning, "Go back to Dolisie. If you stay here, you'll die." It seemed clear that God wanted us to go.

But how? We lacked funds, and people with radios warned that war might break out again.

Then Emmanuel returned to Mossendjo—this time with Craig's letter in hand. Emmanuel knew my heart better than anyone. Because there was no mail access in Mossendjo he said, "Médine, you need to go to Pointe-Noire. You can stay in contact with Craig there."

With my family's encouragement, I decided to go there quickly; Eliser had already returned there. Was God bringing about what I hoped?

27

Hope in the Ruins?

Craig

I had no idea what Médine was thinking. Because I had been so wounded in my first marriage and by parts of the Church, I dared not marry anyone without being sure that God was in it. I had long ago decided that my only recourse was to guard my heart. I cared deeply about Médine, but determined to continue acting only as a brother to a sister, as with other women friends. I was still fasting a day each week to try to keep my heart focused on God.

One day in the fall as I was preparing to teach at church, I felt God's voice: *You need to believe that I want to give you a wife.*

"I don't understand," I protested. "I do trust Your love for me. And don't I pour out everything in my life for You sacrificially?"

But I was too busy over the next month to ponder the question further. Preaching, teaching, grading essays, starting work on my new Acts commentary and meeting with students consumed so much of my time that I was often getting only three hours of sleep a night. Fighting unending fatigue, I just disciplined myself more rigorously. I was positively devoted to God, but I was negatively running from my own heart's pain. I was terrified of my pain catching up with me.

Médine

This time as I traveled to Pointe-Noire by way of Dolisie, I brought David; I had missed him too much the last time and did not know how long I might be away. David, who was nearly three years old, was afraid of the truck when we started, but soon became curious about everything.

While we were in Dolisie, some soldiers heard David calling them Cobras and speaking Kitsangui. "It's good for you that there's a truce on," one of the soldiers spat. "Otherwise we'd kill your little future Cocoye." Praying hard, I secured David firmly to my back with my body cloth and started walking. Sometimes David was too free with his tongue.

Hope for Restoration

After another day in Dolisie to attend church, David and I rode a truck to Lebanda, where we waited all day for a train. We were shivering, drenched by rain. That evening I laid my body cloth on the muddy dirt floor to bed down at the station for the night, holding David close and praying that God would protect us from the cold weather and robbers.

When the train finally pulled into the station, pandemonium erupted as everyone scrambled to find a place on board. I shook out my body cloth, affixed David to my back, lifted my bag and fought my way onto the train.

Because it was dangerous to take the train at night, many who had been waiting elected not to board, somewhat reducing the competition for a place. But I had David and did not want to sleep outside. Soon after the train lurched forward into the night, we were drenched in the blackness of a long, dark tunnel. David was terrified. Back out in the countryside, where the rail line had not been kept up, tree branches whipped us periodically. I clung to David and my bag in the dark.

Upon arriving in Pointe-Noire, I found a cybercafé and was able to email Craig. A couple of days later I returned to find a response from Craig awaiting me, along with instructions to pick up two hundred dollars from Western Union!

Breaking Free

I decided that the first thing to take care of was the divorce. Friends had by now informed me that, even though Manassé had signed documents to marry me monogamously, he already had, by traditional marriage, another wife and children in the same city. "Marrying" me, I assumed, simply gave him ready access to my income. Witnesses informed me that after I left he relocated some of my possessions to the home of his real wife.

Since Manassé had signed for monogamy, our union was illegal, but one way or the other I still needed documentation that I was not married. Traveling around the war-torn country to look for documents to annul the marriage would be dangerous. It was simplest to become legally free from him by filing for divorce again. I did not think it should be a difficult matter; I had been abandoned for three years, and I had already filed for divorce once.

Still, Manassé had taunted me that I would never get free from him. Having other partners, he did not need me for himself, but he knew I could not marry anyone else without legal papers.

"I'll make you suffer alone indefinitely," he had threatened. I picked up the money Craig had wired and gave a lawyer a down payment to file for me again.

That week, in response to a dream, Eliser and I decided to return to Mossendjo, carrying the rest of Craig's money. I planned to return there to take my family to Dolisie.

Craig

I reread often one of Médine's letters that summarized her war experience: "We walked miles and miles in the forest, whether under the scorching sun or torrential rains. We suffered without clean drinking water, toilets and money to buy food. We ate once a day and slept on the ground. Northern soldiers attacked and some southern soldiers also raped and plundered their own people. Yet we saw God heal people in answer to prayers. Many people began to join our prayer times. Hardship draws us closer to God."

Médine had promised me that she would be back in touch by email at a certain time. When I did not hear from her I grew even more anxious for her safety. I knew the country was still unstable and that travel remained dangerous. I could only write, hoping she could receive my email, and urge her to contact me whenever she needed money.

Médine

On one old, crowded truck, I held David as high as I could with one arm to protect him from suffocating, and with my other arm grasped a pole above our heads so that we would not fall off. This truck had to stop four times to refill the radiator with water. By the end of my trip, my arms were aching so badly that I wanted to cry.

Soon after we reached Mossendjo I succumbed to malaria once again. Before I could fully recover, soldiers summoned me to translate some documents for them. One of the documents outlined a northern bombardment plan for cities and towns in the south. Contrary to what the prophecies had stated, these papers indicated that war was coming again.

Though I was told to forget everything I had translated, obviously I could not. I would not broadcast it, but the new information would clearly affect our plans. Dejected, I shared the information with my family, and my parents sadly canceled our immediate plans to return to Dolisie. I gave Emmanuel a letter to mail to Craig. Then I collapsed again with severe diarrhea.

Because there was no more need for travel fares, I bought some real clothes and yogurt to help the family, and some chocolate and bread for the children on David's third birthday in September. But the money was soon running out, and even Papa Jacques's patience was starting to wear thin. I had never before seen him lose hope. This day, however, he grew angry with God. "Why haven't You healed me?" he asked plaintively. "Why are my children all unmarried and unemployed? Why have we become the laughing-stock of everybody, young and old? Where is the most powerful God, the God of the impossible? God—please let me die."

This was the first time that Papa Jacques had questioned God since the war started. That night as we gathered for prayer, as we always did, he cried. "Lord, forgive me for questioning You." Following his example, we all knelt and confessed our lack of sufficient faith and asked God's forgiveness.

Within a few weeks we realized that the documents about war had proved false, but by this time we had no money left for the fares. One day as David was playing in the wheelbarrow, he fell and broke his arm. Lacking funds, all we could do was massage him.

Papa Jacques Sees the Ruins

We set aside three days to pray for an opportunity to return to Dolisie. Finally Papa Jacques was able to arrange with his half-brother Prosper to take us with him on his upcoming trip to Dolisie.

About this time a certain man had begun expressing unwanted interest in me. He was planning to return the next day to visit me again. I was truly hoping we would be gone by then. Prosper had not come to us to confirm the trip, so we all prayed anxiously—myself in particular. Finally at around four o'clock that morning, Prosper's truck rumbled up to our door.

Twelve of us piled in, and eventually we pulled up in front of the remains of our home. Everyone fell silent as our mother was helping Papa Jacques out of the truck. We had told him about the house, but how would he react when with his own eyes he saw his life's work in ashes? For a very intense minute he stared quietly at the ruins. Then he spoke. "Let's thank God. Others lost loved ones. God has protected our lives."

There in front of his ruined house with his family around him, Papa Jacques prayed. "Thank You, Lord, for Your kindness, for protecting our lives during war and for watching over us during the trip." Even though some of us were crying over a lost dress or book, everyone said "Amen" with him. Then my parents walked slowly among the remains of the home they had not seen for some nineteen months.

Punished by God?

We cleaned up the small rooms of the narrow adjoining structure. It would be difficult to fit everyone side by side on the floor at night there, but at least we were in our own community.

I did not plan to stay, however. I had decided to settle with Eliser in Pointe-Noire and look for work there. I felt that I would only be another mouth for my destitute parents to feed if I remained. Besides, the eerie quiet in Dolisie stirred painful memories. Before the war, the neighborhood had been filled with the sounds of precious, happy children playing. Though the adult refugees had now returned, most of those young neighbor children had died. Their silence was too painful to bear.

So the next week I headed again for Eliser's dilapidated dwelling in Pointe-Noire. Yet no jobs were available, especially for refugees. How would I buy bread for David? I began buying charcoal in large bags, then reselling it by the road in smaller bags for a little profit.

The tiny wooden shack David and I were staying in—one in a line of nearly abandoned one-room shacks, including the one in which Eliser stayed—was decrepit; whenever it rained, the tin roof leaked. Meanwhile rainwater flooded in through the door, quickly soaking or setting afloat anything on the ground. My biggest concern during the rains, though, was the leeches that washed into the houses; they could attach to our skin and were not easily removed. I kept my few belongings on the old bed or on some red bricks to minimize water damage. David and I had no sheet to cover us at night other than my body cloth. Soon I passed my 37th birthday, abandoned with a child, jobless and destitute. Though disheartened, I thanked God for being with me.

Later that week I ran into a minister I knew who greeted me warmly. After telling me about his thriving ministry in a nearby village, he asked how I was doing.

"I'm—I'm looking for work right now. . . ."

He shook his head impatiently. "Why didn't you just find a way to stay in France when you finished studying, like other Congolese? Maybe God had an important ministry for you there, and you disobeyed Him by coming back to Congo. That would explain why nothing is working for you—your marriage, employment prospects, having to raise a child on your own." After he had finished preaching to me, he said goodbye and left.

I remained motionless for a long time. I felt guilty and ashamed. My head dropped down as warm tears flooded my cheeks. I started walking painfully, praying and weeping inside, trembling with despair. I did not care that passersby were shaking their heads as they saw me. Those who had mercifully escaped the ravages of war, as Pointe-Noire had, often did not understand those who had been forced to endure it.

But what if he is right? I wondered. *What if I really am being punished by God?*

Was Love Possible?

I also had a new quandary. The post office in Dolisie had survived the war and retained letters that Craig had sent before the war began. Emmanuel brought these to me from Dolisie. The letters were filled with words of affection and concern for me, but no specific romantic intention. In my culture, as I have noted, the man initiates any expression of interest. I had poured out my feelings to Craig in the past and did not feel comfortable approaching the subject again.

When I confided my thoughts to Emmanuel he spoke plainly. "You and Craig are playing a bad game," my brother charged. "It's clear from these letters that you still love each other. You need to tell him your feelings for him. Remember France: Western customs are different. It's not wrong there for a woman to share her feelings."

"I can't," I protested helplessly. The risk of rejection was too great. "I'll just pray."

I did not want to burden Craig with our many needs, but I did write to him that I needed new glasses. After several days I still had not heard from him. Normally he responded to email the same day. Now I was feeling guilty that I had asked for money; did he find that inappropriate? Would it harm our friendship?

That night in a dream a voice assured me: "God is the one who puts love in our hearts. No one can remove that love, for it is strong."

Still, Craig was not responding. Was something wrong?

28

The Day Breaks

Craig

For months I had been heading toward collapse.

In November my body became dehydrated from the uncontrollable heater in the apartment; I had been too busy to ask maintenance to repair it. The week after midterms I spent thirty hours grading essays and papers without reducing my forty to fifty hours of writing and teaching. The day I returned the essays, after teaching for a few hours, I felt overwhelmed, dizzy and sweaty. Turning pale, I nearly fell to the floor.

"I need to finish my lecture," I protested, but I was taken to the hospital anyway.

The cardiologist certified that my heart was fine. I was dehydrated and fatigued, but it was not my physical heart that was the problem. After my release I dove back to work and two days later ended up in the emergency room again. This time I felt as though I was being dragged out of consciousness, slipping down into a bottomless pit. The doctor sedated me so heavily that I spent most of the day asleep. Some friends kept me for a few days at their home because I was now too weak to shower, prepare food—even to walk. Like Médine, though for different reasons, I was also experiencing post-traumatic stress disorder.

Nevertheless I now experienced God's grace in a fresh way. I had been fasting and striving to be ever more pure before Him; there was so much to do for His Kingdom and I had done so little yet. Now I had to learn anew that God loved me and acted on my behalf even when I could not work. I was learning that God's call is His promise, not just a goal for us to achieve.

The medicine knocked me out to the point that I could not stand; I could only crawl. I begged my friends to take me back to the seminary. What if Médine were trying to reach me? That would be a life-and-death matter, too. "I can lie on my own bed as well as on someone else's," I pointed out. "And I don't want the food in my refrigerator to spoil." My friends were afraid that I would try to work again, but they finally complied and took me to my on-campus apartment.

After a day in my efficiency apartment, I persuaded my teaching assistant to locate a moveable chair and push me to the faculty offices where I could check my email. There I crawled up the stairs and to my office. My assistant let me in, and I climbed into my seat. Staring at the computer screen to read even one email message was so difficult that I needed to lie down on the floor again, but I had to see if Médine had written.

Médine had, in fact, written about her need. A friend thus took me to a Western Union desk. Too dizzy to wait in line, I plopped down on the floor until my turn; health takes precedence over social convention.

Médine

I was relieved to get Craig's email but worried about him. With the $470 he sent, I bought glasses, paid the lawyer another installment and enrolled David at an affordable school. I rationed the rest. David needed to learn French because he knew only his village and regional languages, which the family had mostly been speaking as refugees.

David excelled in school but was troubled because each day he saw his classmates being picked up by their fathers. "Where's *my* father?" my three-year-old finally asked.

I swallowed hard. "He's abroad," I answered hopefully. Satisfied, David now talked with his friends about his own father. I prayed that someday he would have a father who really loved him.

When I confided in my friend Julie, she proved as emphatic as Emmanuel: "Write Craig and tell him your feelings."

Yet I was still afraid. The first time we had discussed marriage, seven years before, had been painful. On that occasion, writing from France, I had expressed my feelings carefully and waited for my answer serenely and confidently, certain that it was God's will. But apparently it had not been. Would I ever find the courage again to tell Craig how much I loved him?

I ran into many people I knew who had settled in Pointe-Noire. Mustafa, who was preparing to return to Sierra Leone, was happy to see me. Inspector Pi and I talked about our experiences in Mbomo Center. I also encountered an old friend who had something to confess. "When Manassé proposed to you, he was seeing another woman plus his wife. I was dating Manassé's best friend, and he warned me not to tell you or he'd break up with me."

"Why are you telling me now?" I asked.

"He broke up with me anyway," she complained. "I'm so sorry I never told you."

"It's all right," I comforted her. "It's over now. Don't feel guilty." I felt bad for the other woman that Manassé had deceived also.

I finally decided to settle matters with Craig one way or the other. I also wished desperately that I could nurse him back to health; he obviously was not taking proper care of himself. Finally, a few days after Christmas, I took the advice given me and wrote Craig a letter sharing my feelings with him.

Now came more waiting; the letter would take three weeks to reach him. What would he think? At least I had finally gotten the courage to tell him once more of my love for him. Though I could *feel* his love for me, I imagined that his answer might well be a reluctant no. I resolved that if he responded again that he did not think our marriage likely, I would end our correspondence, leave Pointe-Noire and let time cure my heart. I would forever abandon hope of our impossible love.

Craig

Friends at the seminary brought me food each day until I was able to prepare my own. I realized how lonely a place my apartment—basically an office that I slept and ate and worked in—had become. It was pleasant to have human contact, even if I was receiving rather than imparting grace at the moment. At first I spent most of the day lying on my back, staring at the ceiling. Physically unable to read, I listened to the Bible on tape. For once I wished I had a television. It would be at least half a year before I could even begin reading academic books again, much less writing them.

Forced to slow down, I also discovered that there were people who loved me even if I had nothing to offer them except myself. Eventually I could walk short distances, though I often had to stop and lie down. Over my Christmas break, my parents drove to Philadelphia and brought me to Ohio to rest.

I was determined to keep a ministry commitment at the end of December, but afterward my return journey to Philadelphia was arduous. I was so weak I finally collapsed in the deep snow near the seminary and had to crawl to the door. I slept through most of January.

That was my condition when Médine's letter expressing her love for me arrived.

Had her letter come at any other time, I would have put the question off, too busy to try to obtain divine certainty about such a big decision. Instead I was flat on my back and unable to do much beyond thinking and praying. I had once felt that God was saying no because our incompatibility made romantic love impossible, but I had never felt sure in my inclinations about such matters and always chose to err far on the side of caution. Now I wondered if such a no, even if it was from the Lord, was only temporary—as when God forbade Paul's ministry in Asia in Acts 16 but blessed it there later. In fact, when I had prayed about her again in recent years, Médine was the only woman I knew whom God had not said no to—though He also had not said yes.

To marry someone so dear to me seemed a gift too great to hope for. Fourteen years after being abandoned, I still could not imagine anyone loving me romantically except out of disciplined obedience to God.

My friend Kristin had been mentoring me spiritually since my collapse, so I crawled across the floor to my telephone and filled her in. "I do love Médine," I complained sadly, "and feel excited that she loves me. I'm just so afraid that if I ask God again He is going to say no."

"That's not what I'm hearing Him say," Kristin responded. Kristin had been present when I received Médine's first letter after the war, and from that time had believed, without telling me, that Médine was to be my future wife.

"I don't want to get her hopes up—in case God tells me no. Maybe I should discourage her until I hear for sure," I said. I did not know that Médine had resolved to end contact if she received a discouraging answer from me.

"Don't quench her hope," Kristin warned.

So I sent Médine this suggestion: "Let's keep praying and see what God is saying. *This* time we'll each keep praying till we both hear the same thing."

Once I sent that message by email, I found myself so excited that I did not know how to evade bias. So I reverted to a more objective approach: I would go back over everything God had told me about the person I would marry to see if Médine fit. With what little strength I had, I spent the next few days poring over my journals and the scores of old letters from Médine.

But what heartache that brought! Several times I cried out in anguish. How I had missed the obvious! I finally came to the letter in which she had written, "Ministry is too strong a term for what I do." Yet what she described was the very sort of ministry that in prayer I had felt my future wife was doing. Somehow, over the semantics of the word *ministry*, I had missed it—for seven years.

I fell out of my chair, literally.

Finally I felt I heard God speak. The love I had offered up to God as a sacrifice of obedience to what I thought was His will, He had given back to me as a gift. Once I was convinced that He approved of my having romantic love for Médine, it was like removing the cork from a bottle.

Médine

Three long weeks had passed since I had mailed my letter, and I had heard no response. Perhaps Craig had taken offense and quit corresponding. Still, I went back to the cybercafé to check my email periodically. In deep anguish I finally committed the matter to God. "I want Your will," I prayed, "whether that's a yes or a no."

The next time I stopped in, I discovered Craig's email, sent a few days earlier. I examined it anxiously. Was he angry? No! He said we should pray until we both came to the same conclusion. I knew what I thought was God's will, but I wanted marriage to Craig so much that I feared I was just hearing what I wanted to hear. For now, however, I had hope.

The next day I returned to the cybercafé, just in the unlikely event that he had written again so quickly. Sure enough, there was a new email from Craig. But what did it say? Was it good news this time? Or bad?

Too anxious to wait, I started reading it while I was still paying the clerk. Suddenly my eyes fell across Craig's answer: He had already heard from God, and it was yes! Unable to restrain my joy, I started laughing.

"Have you received some good news from your American brother who always writes to you in English?" the young clerk inquired.

"Yes," I responded and hurried out of the café so happy that I kept on laughing, walking along by myself while reading his email over and over. Onlookers were staring as if to say, *So many people lost their minds during war.* Ignoring them I kept on singing joyfully to God, unable to stop thanking Him.

The next day I emailed him back. Despite my eagerness I wanted to make him aware of some changes. "A lot of my hair fell out during war," I warned, "and what's left is turning gray." Although I would not recommend this for relationships, it had been nearly twelve years since we had seen each other in person. We could not yet see each other, but at least we could soon hear the other say, "I love you." I began traveling an hour each way to homes that had phones so I could receive his calls.

What neither of us knew was that governments do not accede readily to the principles of romance.

29

Leaving Congo?

Médine

I began telling David about his new father-to-be, Papa Craig. David, who had never known a father, grew very happy. Now he would be like the other children in the school! He was so excited, in fact, that he began telling a visitor about Papa Craig. "I have a father who loves me, and his name is Craig," he beamed. Wanting to keep the secret for now, I changed the subject as I laughed with the visitor about children's imaginations.

Craig, however, learned from David's childlike trust. "I, too, have a Father who loves me," he said in celebration. "His name is God."

To apply for visas to the U.S., David and I would first need passports. Although I had kept my passport throughout the war, the new government had invalidated the former government's passports.

My friend Mado had connections at the passport office in Brazzaville. In mid-February, therefore, I entrusted to her the passport fee and all the identification papers for David and myself. "Pray that there aren't any more upheavals," Mado warned, "or I might not get back to Brazzaville to pick up your documents."

Later Mado returned. "They say they need more money," she told me.

I gave her more—but I never saw her again. Surely Mado was trustworthy, so something unexpected must have happened.

In the meantime, crisis struck. To reduce Craig's worry, I had not informed him how bad my conditions were. I remained in Pointe-Noire because this was the only way I could keep in touch with him. David and I still lived in the same ramshackle structures near Eliser. To read after dark, I used a candle; I kept Craig's letters on our old bed to preserve them from the often-flooded floor. I cooked outside. I had to cross the street to get water, which was contaminated. Many people were dying from typhoid; David and I were regularly sick from malaria. At least it was better than the forest.

One day as I returned from the market, I found David convulsing, cold all over and breathing with difficulty. Others had called our family cursed, declaring that we would never have children; David was all that I had. Now that I could finally anticipate marriage, it looked as though I might lose my precious son. I loaded my gasping child onto my back, praying frantically. Grabbing Craig's money, I raced for the nearby infirmary, crying and splashing through puddles of mud. Malaria medicine saved David's life. Many precious children whose families did not have money for medicine died.

Craig

One African American charismatic woman at our seminary sat me down firmly in the seminary lobby. "I have a word from the Lord for you," she announced, and I held my breath in anticipation. Apart from Kristin, who was keeping matters in confidence, very few people knew about my new relationship. "God has now brought the wife you've been praying for," she said, "so you can stop looking. Also, don't worry about the intercultural element." Meanwhile others who did not know each other or the situation also began volunteering similar prophecies.

My spiritual mentors concurred. "I told you that Médine would marry a spiritual warrior," Jackie Reeves said. "I felt that it was you." As I reexamined my journal, I saw that she had actually hinted as much.

How could I have been so blind, I wondered? But then I had a dream. The dream's setting was some seven years earlier, when Médine and I first discussed marriage. Revising history in the dream, I decided to marry Médine before the war, but as I reached the door of my North Carolina apartment, I found that the key did not fit the lock. It was instead my current Philadelphia key. Then the Lord spoke: *It isn't yet time. You're not yet ready.* When I awoke I understood: Seven years earlier, though God already planned for us to be together, that plan was for the future. Seven years before, I could not yet understand the plan because neither of us was ready for what our life together would truly entail. Now was the time.

I drew on other encouragement as well. A few years after the betrayal of my first marriage, I knew beyond doubt that I had forgiven Cass and Oswardo completely—even in my dreams. "I really *am* a Christian," I had laughed to myself when I awoke. At that time I had sent a letter to Cass and Oswardo assuring them that I forgave them fully. For years after that I heard nothing back, assuming that it, like the rose or love letters earlier, had ended up in the trash. Perhaps they still would insist that they had not done anything wrong, and thus regarded my assertion of love and forgiveness as presumptuous. I worried that my letter might have done more harm than good.

But now, fourteen years after she had left me, Cass replied, confessing that she had long been tormented by guilt. "Like Joseph," she said, "you forgave us, even though we didn't apologize. Now it is time for me to face fear and guilt, and apologize."

That letter welcoming my expression of forgiveness was a moment of great healing for me.

I was with you even when you felt most forsaken, God reminded me, *even if you didn't see it then.* I felt God showing me that I was going to see the other side of Hosea, a side I had almost forgotten. Hosea is not just about God's broken heart; it is also about God's restoring love.

Médine

When Thérèse visited, I confided in her about Craig.

"I already knew," Thérèse laughed. "I've been having dreams and visions about it."

I soon received the money Craig sent for my trip abroad, but documents remained an issue. My lawyer assured me that his colleague in Brazzaville had submitted the papers for my divorce—though a prophecy warned that I needed to pray much about that situation. I still had heard nothing from Mado regarding the passports; no one, in fact, seemed to know where Mado was. And the U.S. consulate in Brazzaville was closed due to the war, so once I had the passports in hand I would have to travel to the consulate in Cameroon's capital to obtain our visas.

And I faced other problems. A taxi hit me and injured my foot, where I had already been losing my toenails from malnutrition.

Craig

It was a blow to learn that Médine did not have official divorce papers; like her, I had assumed that her filing before the war had been successful. After some of the harsh criticism I had endured because of my own experience years earlier, I wanted to avoid anything that could even be suspected of dishonor and hence would keep people from hearing my message. In my entire life, I had never kissed anyone except the woman I had married.

One seminary student, Charlemagne Nditemeh, a Cameroonian Baptist, began to discuss the situation with me. Son of a village chief, Charlemagne had investigated religion, become a Christian and eventually led many relatives and much of his village to faith in Christ. Providentially, Charlemagne had studied law at the university and knew the French legal system well. "Ratifying Médine's freedom from such a marriage should be a simple matter," he explained. "No Western legal system would deny it or delay it like this."

Médine's lawyer was a distant relative, but Charlemagne and I began to suspect that he was lying to her.

Médine

I was losing money trying to call the lawyers from roadside phones; they were not responding. Finally, in mid-April, I resolved that I would need to venture into Brazzaville myself to address the passport issue and try to determine what I could about the divorce papers. Craig was panicked for my safety, but I felt the urge to go. Conditions could not be worse than in Pointe-Noire; a storm had just blown our roof off and drenched us there.

Emmanuel had traveled ahead of me and had bad news when I arrived. The immigration office had no passport application on file for me.

215

I could not believe it. I hurried to the office when it reopened. "No one enters without paying me a fee," the guard demanded. I had to pay 1000 CFA (about two dollars). Once inside I scoured the registration book over and over, only to confirm that *there was no record my passport had ever been applied for.* If the paperwork I had sent with Mado, such as my birth certificate, was lost, I might *never* be able to leave the country. It had to be here! I checked again and again. David's name was there, but I simply was not listed in the registry.

I returned to Dr. Mabiala's apartment, where we were staying, utterly spent. What could I do? Without birth certificates we could not get passports, and without passports we could not fly to Cameroon to obtain visas. God had protected my documents throughout the war, and now they were lost.

Craig

Still not fully recovered, I took the news hard. Médine and I had been praying to be reunited within a few weeks. I also felt panicked regarding her safety so long as she remained in Congo. I prayed with Kristin and Rosamund; Rosamund was a Baptist from Ghana who had been praying for Médine's release. As we prayed Rosamund offered this counsel: "I feel that the Lord is saying that the passport is done."

I was exasperated. "It's not done!" I protested. "Don't you understand? That's just the problem! There *is* no passport."

She replied quietly but firmly, "I feel that it *is* done."

Kristin agreed, but I was unbelieving. A Kenyan Pentecostal brother also said to me, "It's done; I feel sure." Someone else had said she felt the passport materials were in a file in someone's desk. I was fed up with this subjective, unrealistic charismatic nonsense. I told Rosamund's prophecy to Médine, but I felt completely overwhelmed.

Médine

"It has to be there," I insisted to Craig desperately. "God wouldn't bring us this far to abandon us." In the morning I showed up at the immigration office again. "No one enters without paying me a fee," the guard repeated.

"I gave you one thousand francs yesterday, and that's it," I insisted. "You're not getting any more." The man stormed inside angrily, but since I continued to stand outside, saying nothing, he finally waved me in. The official who was supposed to help me completely ignored me, taking care of people only from his own region.

After two hours, noticing that no one was helping me, the receptionist scribbled down a name. "Go find this man on the second floor and see if he can help." I hurried to that man's office.

"I don't have time for this," the man responded, "but go see my colleague."

I entered that office timidly. "Your colleague sent me to see you, sir."

"Ah, welcome. What may I help you with?"

"Sir, I sent all my documents by a friend to file for passports for my son and me," I explained. "But my friend disappeared, and I've found only my son's name in the register and no passport at all."

"What's your name?" he asked, seeming interested.

"Médine Moussounga," I replied hopefully.

"Ah, well, that's why your face appears so familiar. Your passport has been sitting in my drawer for a long while. Why didn't your friend come back?" He pulled my passport from his drawer and had me sign it. I thanked him, and in my heart thanked God who had guided me to the very person who *had* my passport. I learned later that Mado, who had done her work faithfully, had fallen sick and was unable to leave the village.

Now I just needed to find the lawyer, Maitre Bouka, to see about the divorce. Despite warnings from people of prayer, a few days later everything seemed resolved. "I don't have all the signatures just yet," he assured me, "but the divorce *has* gone through. Here, I'll give you an affidavit to that effect." I felt confident about the document he handed me as proof of my divorce; Charlemagne had assured Craig and me that no lawyer would dare issue a false affidavit for fear of losing his license.

Craig

The passports in hand, Médine traveled with David to Cameroon the next week to secure the visas. For years I had meticulously conserved money, living on the barest amount so I could serve needs in Africa. I had read that a dollar could provide daily meals for several children, and the price of my background commentary could be a month's wages for an average pastor.

I had saved some for a wedding; I would now need it instead for expenses for Médine and David and for our transatlantic flights. At this point she needed just her visa and the final paperwork regarding her divorce. I booked my ticket for Cameroon.

Médine

Charlemagne's friend Samuel worked for the Cameroonian government, and he and his wife, Adama, welcomed me to stay with them until I could get the visas to go to the U.S. I was astonished at the guest room. It was spacious, with a real bed and concrete floors.

On a Monday in May 2001, Craig and I saw each other in person for the first time in nearly twelve years. He had told me that he rarely slept on planes, so he arrived in Yaoundé, Cameroon's capital, pale and dizzy, not fully recovered from

218

his collapse. I scanned the faces eagerly and recognized him immediately—the most handsome man there.

Craig

It was like a wonderful dream. Finally I was reunited with my dear friend and future wife, Médine! I had brought a ball, and after my first night of sleep (Samuel had an additional guest room) I started playing with three-year-old David. "Throw the ball," I explained as I tossed it to him, beginning to teach him English. He learned the alphabet in two days, and learned quickly to count and spell in English.

He confided to Médine in French one day, "Papa Craig is not very good with French . . . but his English is *quite* good."

We were growing anxious, however, because the lawyer still had not sent the final paperwork regarding her divorce. On June 11 the devastating truth came out. Dr. Mabiala's brother-in-law Timothée, a military officer, with the help of a state prosecutor, discovered that Médine's lawyer had never filed for the divorce.

In the sight of the law, she was still married.

30

International Affairs

Craig

We were horrified and ashamed. Médine and I had both been careful not to walk in any way that could give anyone reason to question our integrity. Had we been so careful all these years, at enormous cost, only to invite dishonor now?

As we prayed, I felt God speaking: *The way is hard because I am cutting a new way before you, clearing a new path for you through the stubborn rocks. You don't know the future—but you know My character. Look to the future not with fear, but as a challenge, as when I told Israel to take their land. For I am with you.*

Even the devil and his plans, God reminded us, were ultimately subject to God's will.

Yet more days passed, and again the Lord had to calm my anxiety. *It's not you, My child, who must bring My word to pass. Peter struck with a sword, thinking that he was fighting for Me; I will defend My own honor.*

But how would He do so? It seemed that one problem after another kept blocking our way.

Médine had no choice but to try once more either to obtain documentation of Manassé's bigamy or to finalize the divorce. Finally she decided that she would have to return to Brazzaville to address the situation directly. Hearing reports of continued instability in Congo, I was fearful again for her safety.

I could not go with her. My lawyer warned that under U.S. policy for fiancée visas, I had to return to the U.S. and visit her again only after she returned to Cameroon with the proper papers. I agreed with starting over; this needed to be settled before we could be properly engaged.

A further heartbreak was that she did not dare take David back into a dangerous area, so *neither* of us could be with him. She would have to leave him with Samuel's family. This all meant a few thousand unanticipated dollars for flights, more delays— and trauma for a little boy who had already suffered so much.

Médine

After we saw Craig off at the airport, I talked with David. "Mommy is going to have to leave you here for a while." He seemed cooperative, but did he really understand how long I might be gone? A few days later I bade David farewell at the airport. He was crying and could not understand that it would be days before he would see me again.

I called him from the airport in Douala. He was still crying. "Where are you? Please come back quickly."

"I have to be away for a few more days," I explained, but he seemed not to understand. My heart was breaking when I hung up. Now separated from his new father, his always-constant mother and everyone he knew, David cried nightly that his mother had abandoned him and would never come back to him.

A Crooked Lawyer

Email had not been working, so the Mabialas were surprised when I showed up once more at their apartment in Brazzaville. It so happened that Timothée, the police captain, was dining with them. "I threatened to arrest your lawyer," Timothée reported, "but he protested that you hadn't paid him and promised he'd do your file soon anyway."

I drew a folder from my bag and laid out various receipts in front of him. "I didn't just pay him," I said. "I paid him three times over to get the job done."

There were gasps of astonishment around the table. "We'll visit your lawyer tomorrow morning," Timothée promised gruffly, after an uncomfortable pause. "And I'll be wearing my military uniform."

I exhaled. It was no coincidence that I had found Timothée within half an hour of my arrival in Brazzaville.

"And I know an honest lawyer who can help you," Henriette Mabiala assured me. I nevertheless slept anxiously that night, mostly worried about David.

The next day Timothée and I walked into the lawyer's office, catching him off guard. "Uh . . . er . . . I thought you were out of the country, Madame," Maitre Bouka said. "Please come in."

"So I didn't pay you?" I charged, holding up my receipts.

"Madame, I have financial problems and a family to take care of," he protested.

"So you take care of them by wronging a poor woman with a small child? I want my file."

Glancing warily at Timothée, the lawyer reluctantly withdrew the file from his desk yet resisted handing it over. "Let me introduce it in the court," he offered. "This time I'll do it for free."

"I don't trust you anymore."

He lowered his head, ashamed. "You're right," he admitted. "If I were you, I wouldn't trust me either. You see, Madame, a lie is like a tunnel. Once you get inside, it's difficult to turn around."

He handed me the file, and I began checking the contents. When I gazed up at him and saw just how miserable he looked, my anger subsided. He had cost us a lot of money, and the false affidavit he gave me could have gotten him disbarred, but I felt pity for him, trapped in his prison of lies and guilt.

That night I was relieved to talk with Craig by phone, but my heart ached for David. How was he doing? Was he crying? Who was taking care of him when Adama was not there? "Please, Lord, watch over my baby," I cried.

Wonderful News at Last

The next morning Henriette took me to see the honest lawyer. "I'm already familiar with your situation. You need pay only the filing fees," he offered kindly. "I won't charge you anything myself. This should be quick—I'll explain that you submitted your file last year but that the lawyer was corrupt. Just in case there's a short delay, though, you may as well visit your family in Dolisie."

Before traveling to Dolisie I phoned David. "Where are you?" he demanded. "Why aren't you coming back?" He started crying and then the connection cut off, as international phone connections often did. Hot tears ran down my cheeks; there was no way for me to comfort him. "Please, Lord," I prayed, "take care of my little David."

When I visited my family, Thérèse prophesied. "I'll cut a path for you through stones," the prophecy said, reminding me of what Craig prophesied. "There will be a great party in heaven on the day of your wedding; angels will sing even if the ceremony looks simple to you. Your going to the U.S. will have a great impact there." She prophesied further about our ministry, and about Africans evangelizing Europe and North America.

On the appointed day, I anxiously called the new lawyer. "I've just seen a miracle," he announced. "Because of the circumstances, the Moungali court accepted your file immediately and pronounced the divorce. The papers will be ready at the end of the week."

I was elated. I also savored my remaining moments with each member of my family, especially with Papa Jacques. Would I ever see him again?

Once I returned to Brazzaville, saying goodbye again to my big brother, Emmanuel, was particularly difficult. But the time had come for me to embark on a new phase of life.

I phoned from the airport as soon as I landed in Cameroon. "David, I'm back!"

"Mommy, are you coming? Are you really?" Then he left the phone. I cringed; maybe David thought that I was never going to come back to him. Our reunion, however, and Craig's upcoming return to Cameroon were two joyful events that blinded us to the further difficulties ahead.

Craig

Given the high incidence of HIV in Congo, Manassé's promiscuity and Médine's injection from a used needle, we remained concerned about her health. Millions of Africans were infected, many as innocently as Médine could have been, but U.S. policy at that time did not allow HIV-infected immigrants to enter the country.

Médine tried to dismiss my concerns about the possibility of HIV infection, but I discovered that she was not as calm as she pretended to be: After the test, she fainted.

We got the results that same afternoon. Médine approached me solemnly and handed me the slip as my heart pounded. *Negatif*, it proclaimed, and we celebrated.

We would have married right away in Cameroon, but we learned that *marriage* visas would take twice as long as *fiancée* visas to process. Thus I had to return alone to the U.S. at the end of the summer to resume teaching and to file the fiancée visa request.

Médine

I managed to hold back my tears fairly well, but David began weeping as soon as Craig got into the car to go to the airport. Our hosts in Cameroon were patient, but no one expected matters to take this long. Far from my family as well as Craig, I felt more isolated now than during the war.

Craig

My attorney began readying the paperwork, but before he could submit it, the terrorist attacks of 9/11 occurred, taking nearly three thousand lives on American soil. Immigration policy changed overnight.

Along with the terrible impact of the attacks, I was already reeling from news out of Jos, Nigeria, that had come a few days earlier. On September 7, jihadists had begun slaughtering Christians and burning churches, hacking pastors to death in front of their families. This in turn launched a series of reprisals between some younger Christians and Muslims that together would kill some three thousand people over the next year.

Now that jihad had assaulted my own country, I hoped the devastating events of 9/11 might generate interest in Nigeria's plight, and I tried to raise awareness. One sympathetic journalist responded that Americans were just not interested in African stories that did not directly affect U.S. interests.

I loved my brothers and sisters there. I knew that their lives were at risk and wanted to join them, offering my life alongside theirs. And should I die with them, then perhaps an American's death would finally open more Americans' eyes to the suffering there.

When I shared my burdened heart with Médine, she was clear in her response: "Have you lost your mind?" she cried.

Since she was still traumatized by war herself, I knew that she was worried about me. I acquiesced.

But we were not much closer to being together. Our next setback came when an anthrax scare temporarily shut down the Vermont Service Center, where her visa requests were being processed. More months passed. I flew to Cameroon to be with Médine and David during my winter break in December and January. Meanwhile my colleague Ron Sider asked our senator's office to check on Médine's file.

While I was in Cameroon we received good news: Once the senator had explained the situation, Immigration and Naturalization Services approved my request for a fiancée visa and would cable its decision to the consulate. Armed with this notice from the INS, Médine and I visited the consulate at the end of December.

"We cannot accept this," the consul apologized politely. "We need to have the original by diplomatic pouch from the State Department."

We explained our situation, but it did not help.

"The INS must have lost your file," a consular officer explained.

Later an INS official countered with his own charge: "The consulate must have lost it," he said. "You'll have to start the process over."

How was this possible? We had bought our tickets for a return flight to Philadelphia. Our wedding was scheduled. Now we were facing possibly six more months of waiting.

Médine

Because I needed to be living in a country with a functioning U.S. consulate, I was again captive to international politics. Though no longer a war refugee, for most of the previous seven months I had remained further from loved ones than during the war.

"God will make a way for us to go with you, Craig," I insisted. "I have to believe that." But time was running out.

Craig

David, four years old, and I were now attached, and he did not want me to leave without him again. He began to cry when he heard that I would be leaving soon. "Who will play with me?" he cried plaintively in French. The day before my flight, he kept promising, "I will go to Philadelphia with you tomorrow."

"We might not be able to do that," I explained, choking up.

"Please, I want to come with you," he cried. "Don't leave me again."

I was angry at the situation, but God urged us to leave the matter with Him. On the last possible occasion before my departure, we checked with the consulate once more.

"The official paperwork still hasn't arrived," the officer reported solemnly.

Desperate, I lifted David up to the window. "Can you explain to my son why his father is going to have to leave him again?" David, not understanding my English, smiled at the kindly woman, and she wilted. But that could not change protocol.

Everyone at the seminary was waiting for us to return together, but I returned alone and we missed our wedding date. We would have rescheduled it—if we could have known when Médine would get her visa.

Médine

I sobbed much of the day after Craig left. Throughout February, David kept protesting, "Why isn't God answering our prayers?" He finally concluded, "God's not nice." Craig and I felt helpless in the face of his suffering.

I kept urging Craig to speed things up, though I knew there was nothing more he could do. His anxiety continued to inhibit his own physical recovery.

Life grew more difficult for all of us during this extended delay. David was always scared when he was dropped off after school because the neighbor's large dog chased him. One day I heard him screaming in terror as the dog began chasing him, and I ran out and chased the dog. From then on, I took a taxi and brought him home directly.

"They'll let us go," David assured me one day. Two days later it was time to check back with the consulate.

"How are you today?" the agent inquired.

"I can't answer that yet," I responded anxiously.

"Well, I have bad news from the INS," the agent remarked; apparently the original documents still had not arrived. My heart sank, but the agent continued. "We've nevertheless decided to process your case, given your special circumstances."

The next week, eight months after Craig had first come to Cameroon for us, David and I, our new visas in hand, boarded a flight for Philadelphia.

Craig

The resolution happened so fast, after so many months of waiting, that I could not believe it as Médine and David, almost first through the line, ran to greet me. Seminary students and staff were on hand to welcome them.

David could not wait to get to my apartment to see where his own bedroom would soon be and to play with the toy cars I had promised him. He had used discarded plastic as a toy car in Congo, and in Cameroon he had just the few toys I brought in my bags. Now he had more toys than he had ever seen before, gifts not only from me but also from children of seminary students.

I introduced Médine and David to my Revelation class, which had been praying for them. That Saturday I introduced them to the few thousand worshipers gathered at my church.

Because I had spent my wedding savings on travel, we decided to have a private wedding in Kristin's office. Instead, as a gift to us, staff and students at Eastern Seminary planned a beautiful ceremony. My Nigerian friend Emmanuel Itapson returned from his doctoral work to be my best man, and Charlemagne and other friends joined in the wedding.

Six days after Médine and David's arrival, and three years to the day after the family's desperate flight from Moubotsi to Mbomo Center, Kristin, who is a Presbyterian minister, performed our wedding in the seminary chapel; Alyn Waller, my pastor, also contributed. It was a simple wedding. We did not have white dresses or tuxedos; we wore matching Cameroonian garments, a gift from a church where we had ministered. We testified for perhaps an hour about God's goodness to us. For days many people told us (as perhaps they tell all newlyweds) that this was one of the most beautiful weddings they had ever seen. We all felt the presence of God's Spirit.

This climax reminded me of what I had heard from the Lord that helped sustain us through the long months of trying to bring Médine and David to America. He had told me:

> When your strength seems at an end, you see only the beginning of My strength. When your faith is at its end, My kindness has just begun. The time you thought Me farthest, I was there

embracing your pain. This is your God who shows Himself true, the God of the cross. I, who have brought you now to this time, call you to look back and to see My exquisite handiwork, to recognize My design, so you may trust Me. The sea is vast; but it is not vast enough to begin to contain My boundless love for My children, nor to contain all the wisdom of My purposes. My giving love to you is greater than all the sands of the seashore, more vast than the seas, higher than the mountains, more awesome than the skies.

Then He traced examples of His kindness through biblical history and concluded:

But many other stories are not recorded there. Your story is likewise part of the larger story of My work in the world. Each of My children has a story, part of the larger story I am weaving in history. As I will not lose track of the sand of the sea, so I do not lose track of any of My children.

That is why we wanted to use our wedding to tell our story: to remind everyone who would listen that God has purposes in all our lives. He has been writing a special story in all our lives, a story that we understand fully only when we see it in the larger context of God's plan of salvation for all who trust Him.

Craig and Médine

This book recounts, in fact, only a portion of what God has done in our lives. The miraculous and prophetic experiences told here are only a piece of our story. Miracles are a wonderful foretaste of the future Kingdom, but they are merely a sample, sparks of the future. They are not meant to be a panacea for all the world's sufferings.

What goes deeper than miracles is the mystery of the cross. That God can transform this harshest of tragedies, this epitome of brutal human injustice, reminds us that He has a plan even in the heart of suffering. Even the climax of the world's rebellion against Him does not nullify His plan. If God can be found even in the cross—indeed, *especially* there—then we can trust God's plan for us in our own stories, even if they are filled with deep pain and brokenness.

In light of the resurrection, the beginning of a new creation, the cross reminds us that our pain is also God's pain, that He is with us in this world, and that hope in Him transcends any present suffering. In Christ and by the Spirit, God really is with us.

Epilogue

Médine

The wedding makes a fitting climax for the book, but of course life goes on. We celebrate but also are ordinary people with ordinary marriage struggles, plus cross-cultural ones.

Craig

Happily, when I went off the medicine given me after I collapsed, I discovered that the medicine itself had caused much of my stupor. But our new apartment on campus was too small for David to play loudly and me to concentrate on my detailed scholarly work at the same time. After nine more years at Palmer Seminary, we moved into our first house when I took a teaching position and Médine took a pastoral care ministry position at Asbury Seminary. Médine wanted a house; I wanted instead to give the money to missions. We discovered quickly that both the house's former owners and our current next-door neighbors had been missionaries in Congo-Kinshasa and were friends with Papa Jacques's friend Jacques Vernaud. Most of the sellers' proceeds from the sale of the house went to missions. David is now a worship leader and a music major at Asbury University.

Médine

As an African woman, I wanted children more than anything, but age and war had weakened my body; we had only miscarriages. Later, however, my precious eleven-year-old niece, Keren, joined us from Congo. Keren, named for one of Job's daughters after his restoration, was born the week that Craig and I decided to marry. She arrived here the same week in 2012 that Craig received the first volume of his four-volume Acts commentary, which he had started writing a few months before her birth.

Craig

I had left Missouri brokenhearted, feeling rejected by the denomination that had first nurtured me. In time, however, they welcomed my ministry so warmly that those wounds healed. The day that I was visiting an old friend who was now the denomination's general secretary, he noted, "I don't know if you've heard, but we voted to change our policy on divorce for special circumstances like yours. In fact, my office approved the first case based on the new policy *today*." I was stunned: 21 years after my own sad experience, I was present in the very office on the very day that the policy that once excluded me from that denomination's ministry was reversed.

Médine

We paid for Thérèse, Aimé and Eliser to study at a seminary in Cameroon. In the years that followed the war, some of our fellow refugees passed away, including Pastor Nziengue and Dr. Kaya. In at least some cases, the physical trauma of war probably hastened their decline.

In the summer of 2008, it looked as if Papa Jacques was going to die, so we traveled to Congo to spend time with the family.

Craig

At this time I met many people in Médine's story, who were just as she had described them. Papa Jacques was not able to speak much now, but he was thrilled as I shared with him that we were writing Médine's story, partly using her journal, and were going to dedicate the book to him and Mama Jacques. "I share your testimonies with my students and others," I noted. "My students are deeply touched when I recount how you praised God even when you saw your house destroyed. Maybe you thought that your life's work was mostly finished. But it's not true: Your ministry is now touching the United States." He spent most of each day sitting in his chair in the narrow building that had survived war. Yet as we shared such good news with him, he was overwhelmed with joy, laughing and lifting his hand to the Lord.

While we were there, Thérèse called with news from Cameroon. On this day, as the rest of us gathered for prayer, the three seminarians called to announce that they had been ordained. Papa Jacques had prayed for one of his children to be in ministry; now he had several. I felt honored to be present as God was now vindicating him after his sufferings.

While we were there, Médine showed me many of the sites in her story: where the bullet that had just missed Papa Jacques had come from; where the Angolan soldiers had stopped Aimé; the Bridge Market where the gun battle occurred; where Mama

Jacques realized they had forgotten Papa Jacques's medicine; where the family had found Aimé in Hammar; and so forth. In Brazzaville, the capital, I saw the inside of the apartment where Médine and others hid under furniture during bombing outside; where Emmanuel's car had stalled fleeing the airport; and the airport and the train station.

When I would bring up any scene in Médine's story, the family would immediately chime in, each one adding his or her own recollections of the same events. Lud now knew enough English to help Médine with translation. Even the scenes hardest for me to visualize, like crossing the river on a narrow rail, they were able to explain. They reminded me of details that Médine originally forgot to tell me. The family even gladly reenacted some dramatic scenes for me to photograph.

In a brief visit to Kinshasa, we also met Papa Jacques's old friend Jacques Vernaud, who was pastoring a megachurch there. He had not seen Papa Jacques since Médine was very small. He prayed God's blessing on us and on Papa Jacques.

After our visit, Papa Jacques's health improved significantly. During the following summer, he recovered enough strength to speak, declaring happily to everyone that soon he would be with Jesus. There was no malice in his heart toward anyone, including those who had neglected or abused him. On July 4, 2009, Papa Jacques received his greatest wish, to see his Lord.

Just short of six years later, Mama Jacques experienced unexpected abdominal pains; a day later she passed. All six children regathered to honor her as she was buried beside her beloved husband.

God also opened the way for Médine and me to minister together again in Francophone Africa. Most dramatically, in summer of 2012 we taught about ethnic reconciliation to seventeen hundred pastors in postwar Côte d'Ivoire, and so far an estimated eighteen thousand copies of our booklet on ethnic reconciliation have been distributed to pastors in Francophone Africa. God knows the future into which He calls us. No matter what the hardships along the way, He is truly worthy of all our trust. He really is the God of impossible love.

Médine Moussounga Keener, Ph.D., University of Paris 7, is Community Formation Pastoral Care coordinator at Asbury Theological Seminary and has taught French at Asbury University and Eastern University. She wrote her dissertation related to African American women's history and has published various articles in *Dictionary of African Christian Biography* and articles on women in Africa and on other subjects. She co-authored with Craig *Reconciliation for Africa*, a booklet on ethnic reconciliation used in many countries in Africa. Both in Francophone Africa and in the United States, she has publicly shared her experiences of war and reconciliation. Her hobbies include cooking, gardening and putting up with Craig's humor.

Craig S. Keener, Ph.D., Duke University, at http://www.craig keener.com/, is F. M. and Ada Thompson Professor of Biblical Studies at Asbury Theological Seminary. He is author of seventeen books, five of which have won awards in *Christianity Today*. He has also written more than seventy academic articles, several booklets and more than 150 popular-level articles. One of his books, *The IVP Bible Background Commentary: New Testament*, now in a second edition, has sold more than half a million copies. His books include commentaries on Matthew, Romans, First and Second Corinthians, Revelation, a two-volume commentary on John and a four-volume commentary on Acts, plus a two-volume work on miracles, works about the

Spirit, ethnic reconciliation, women in ministry, divorce and various other topics. His publishers include Baker Academic, Cambridge, Eerdmans, InterVarsity, Zondervan and others. Craig is the New Testament editor (and author of most New Testament notes) for *The NIV Cultural Backgrounds Study Bible*. In his spare time, he draws silly cartoons and writes Christian songs. Unlike his son, David, however, he does not dare try to sing in front of anybody.